Tiferet

FOSTERING PEACE THROUGH LITERATURE & ART

ISSN: 1547-2906
ISBN: 978-0-578-59963-2

Tiferet

AUTUMN/WINTER 2019

FOUNDER & PUBLISHER
Donna Baier Stein

EDITOR-IN-CHIEF
Donna Baier Stein

MANAGING EDITOR
Lisa Sawyer

POETRY EDITOR
Adele Kenny

PROSE EDITOR
Jeremy Birkline

ASSOCIATE EDITORS
Pamela Walker
Jane Ebihara

CONTRIBUTING EDITORS
Nancy Lubarsky
Priscilla Orr
Bob Rosenbloom

DESIGNERS & ILLUSTRATORS
Donna Schmitt
Monica Gurevich-Importico

STAFF INTERNS
Anu Mahadev
Elinor Bonifant
Mariel Zena
Matthew Green
Natalie Hirt
Peter Henry
Sasha Starovoitov

COVER ART
"Images from Ecuador: Chakana Series" by Sarah Shepley

Donor Honor Roll

Heartfelt thanks to the following donors/co-publishers who donated to help publish this special issue on the theme of Borders:

$0-$99

Alison Knapman
Alison Morse
All Weather Music
Amanda Marcott-Thottunkal
Ami Kaye
Amy Bartow-Melia
Amy Small-McKinney
Amy Van Allen
Anna Weber
Anne McCrady
Anneliese Schultz
Anonymous
Antoinette Libro
Anu Mahadev
Astrid Fitzgerald
Ava Haymon
Aviva Siegel
Barbara Adler
Basil Rouskas
Benjamin Coonley
Beth Paulson
Betsy Woodman
Betti Kahn
Beverly Brodsky
Bonnie Coulter
Brad Miller
Bradford Bedar
Bridget A Nutting
Bruce Goss
Carine Topal
Carol Sanders
Carole Newlands
Caryn McLaine

Catherine Leverenz
Charles DeFanti
Charmian Woodhouse
Christie Cochrell
Christopher Niedt
Concetta Moore
Cynthia Keyworth
Cynthia Peabody
Dallas Itzen
David Fittipaldi
David Hanig
David Thibodeau
David Williams
Dawn Raffel
Deborah Bayer
Deborah DeNicola
Deborah Osredker
Debra Michels
Deena Linett
Dennis Hallinan
Diane Bonavist
Donna Stein
Dorothy Rice
Dorothy Ryan
Elaine Durbach
Emily Rufino
Florence Shelso
Floyd Kemske
Francisco Zuniga
Gail Gerwin
Georgiana Nelsen
Geraldine Miller
Gladys Swan

Donor Honor Roll

$0-$99

Hannah Gross
Hazel Saville
Helen Woodman
Helena Lipstadt
Ian Evans
Ina Roy Faderman
Jack Zellner
Jacqueline L. Robinson
Jaime Pineda
Jamaal Ferguson
James Keane
Jan Brogan
Jan Presley
Jane Ebihara
Jane O'Shields-Hayner
Jane Schulman
Janice Eidus
Jeanne Larsen
Jennifer Aaron
Jennifer Begin
Jennifer Clements
Jennifer Hand
Jennifer Hollis
Jennifer Thibodeau
Jesse Hoffmann
Jessica Segall
Joan Daidone
Joanne Alfano
Joanne O'Brien
John Archer
John Cioffi
John Edward Hasse
JudIth Gaietto-Grace
Judith Sherrard
Juliana Jacobson
Julie Maloney

Karen Bookman Kaplan
Karl Francis Segall
Katherine Hauswirth
Katherine Soniat
Kathleen Petranech
Kathryn Ridall
Kelly Ramsdell
Kenneth Knapman
Kerry Haselton
Kevin James
Kim Buskala
Laine Sutton Johnson
Laura Melmed
Laura Rosenthal
Laurel McHargue
Lawrence Ballon
Lee Woodman
Leslie McGrath
Lia Di Stefano
Linda Leschak
Linda Stryker
Linda Swanberg
Linda Woznicki
Lisa Jordan
Lisa Orlick
Lisa Sawyer
Lisa Sturm
Lois P Jones
Lori Martinez
Lucinda Gadow
Lynda R Myers
Lynne Rathgeber
Marcia Jacobs
Marcia Slatkin
Margaret Stiassni-Sieracki
Maria Gillan

Donor Honor Roll

$0-$99

Marilyn Mohr
Marjorie Swett
Mark Hillringhouse
Mark P. and Arlyn Miller
Mary Beth Kirchner
Matt Maxwell
Maureen Meshenberg
Mel Leshinsky
Melissa Kirkpatrick
Mi West
Michael Cooper
Michael Fontana
Michael Kosoy
Michael Orlando Yaccarino
Michelle Ortega
Mindy Ohringer
Miriam Katsikis
ML Liebler
Mr KH Graser
Mr P Saville
Nan Becker
Nancy Murray
Nancy Schlosser
Naresh Chandra Saxena
Natalie Hirt
Pamela Davis
Pamela Erens
Pamela Walker
Parthenia Marie Hicks
Pat Whalen
Patricia Hoban-Rich
Paul Carlson
Peter Noterman
Priscilla Orr
Raechel Bratnick
Ray Cicetti

Regina A Davey
Rhonda Wiley-Jones
Rochelle Rio-Glick
Ronald Pies
Ronna Wineberg
Rosalind Stevenson
Ross McKie
Ryder Ziebarth
Salty Loeb
Sandell Morse
Sandra Duguid
Sandra Dvergsdal
Sarah Toth
Scott Lipanovich
Sean Breckenridge
Shannon Lockhart
Sharleen Leahey, songs4peace
Sharon Ingraham
Shirley Mitchell
Stephanie Cowell
Steve Butcher
Steve Davison
Steven Bakur
Stuart Terman
Susan Balik
Susan Tweit
Susanna Ward Saltini
Talia Carner
Tanya Brooking
Terese Svoboda
Terin Miller
Terri Gordon
Tina Minkowitz
Valeria Collins
Victoria Kaloss
Virginia Schultz

Donor Honor Roll

$0-$99

Wendy Gonzalez-Baez
Wendy Wolf
William O'Daly

William Peters
Word Walker Press
Yiskah Rosenfeld

$100-$249

Andrea Jarrell
Anne Harding Woodworth
Basabi Basu
Dani Antman
David Tornabene
Denise Fleissner
Diane Kresh
John Gray
John McDermott
Julie Stuckey
Karen Adey
Kathleen Grimaldi
Lance Mushung

Louise Moriarty
Lucinda Gadow
Marie Hellinger
Mary Marino
Michael Rennie
Michele Daniel
Paul Genega
Peter Smoluchowski
Ray Landy
Susan Clampitt
Thelma Zirkelbach
Tobi Watson
Tom McMillian

$250-$499

Diane Masucci
Kate Petranech

$500-$999

Ann Parker
Ashima Hosalkar

$1000+

Lawrence V. Stein
Susan Jackson

FEATURED COVER ARTIST: SARAH SHEPLEY

Images from Ecuador: Chakana series

Sarah Shepley holds a BFA in art and is an ordained Interfaith chaplain/minister. A professional artist for over 25 years, Sarah has worked as a jeweler, bookmaker, and now as a printmaker.

In 2001, Sarah began her journey through ministry, becoming a student at Bangor Theological Seminary and eventually becoming ordained through The Chaplaincy Institute of Maine in 2011. During her years in school, Sarah became a hospice volunteer and co-facilitated bereavement support groups through AHCH and served 3 months in a CPE program through CMMC. She began volunteering at the Center for Wisdom's women for her internship.

In 2013, Sarah served on the faculty at the Chaplaincy Institute of Maine for two years and continues to offer workshops in art and spirituality.

In 2012, Sarah traveled to Cuba on an Arts and culture trip through Global exchange. The experience opened a door and the following year, she traveled to the Dominican Republic with Partners For Rural Health as a chaplain. Since her trip to the D.R. she has committed her time to studying Spanish in both Central and South America. She traveled to Medellin Columbia in 2015 and discovered an orphanage where there was no art available to the children. From that point on, Sarah has worked to combine her skills as an artist as well as chaplain. Presently, she has developed The Ecuadorian Arts Initiative, a project which serves the creative needs of children throughout Ecuador through teaching art and making donations of materials.

While in the states, Sarah teaches printmaking and booking classes while exploring the medium of geli printmaking. Many of her pieces are inspired by her travels to South America and all sales go directly into the project. For more information about her work and the Ecuadorian Arts Initiative visit www.sarahshepley.com.

Tiferet

FOSTERING PEACE THROUGH LITERATURE & ART

TIFERET CAN...

Inspire you to write

Connect you to a global community

Lead toward peace in you and in the world

SUBSCRIBE TODAY to enjoy beautiful, inspiring poetry, fiction, creative nonfiction, interviews and visual art from some of today's best writers.

PAST CONTRIBUTORS INCLUDE:

ROBERT BLY	JEAN HOUSTON	ROBERT PINSKY
RAY BRADBURY	STEPHEN DUNN	ED HIRSCH
ILAN STAVANS	ALICIA OSTRIKER	JANE HIRSHFIELD

and so many more . . . Pulitzer Prize winners to newcomers!

You are welcome to submit your own work (*poems, stories, essays, interviews and visual art*) for us to consider for publication. We also run an annual Writing Contest and award $1500 in prizes. **More details can be found at www.tiferetjournal.com.**

Tiferet: Fostering Peace though Literature & Art is published twice a year in print and digital formats. We read only electronic submissions made through our website submission feature; submissions made through email attachments or by postal delivery will not be considered.

SUBSCRIPTION INFORMATION: Receive two large volumes per year in your choice of print or digital format.

One Year Subscription	$24.95/two print or $18.95/two digital
Two Year Subscription	$39.95/four print or $35.95/four digital
Three Year Subscription	$59.95 /six print or $54.95/six digital
Single Print Issue	$15.00 + $2.50 S&H

U.S. currency (cash or check) and Visa, Mastercard, American Express are accepted. For international delivery, extra charges will apply. Please inquire.

ALL OTHER CORRESPONDENCE MAY BE DIRECTED TO:

Tiferet Journal
211 Dryden Road
Bernardsville, NJ 07924

editors@tiferetjournal.com
www.tiferetjournal.com

ISSN 1547-2906 © 2019 TIFERET JOURNAL AUTUMN/WINTER 2019

Contents

• • • •

> "Thank you for this journal which combines spiritual issues, imaginative issues, esthetic issues. All of those, I think, need to be in the mix for the richly lived life, the richly observed life."
>
> – MOLLY PEACOCK, *former President of the Poetry Society of America*

POETRY

Ancestry

Fred LaMotte

My DNA results came in.
Just as I suspected, my great great grandfather
was a monarch butterfly.
Much of who I am is still wriggling under a stone.
I am part larva, but part hummingbird too.
There is dinosaur tar in my bone marrow.
My golden hair sprang out of a meadow in Palestine.
Genghis Khan is my fourth cousin,
but I didn't get his dimples.
My loins are loaded with banyan seeds from Sri Lanka,
but I descended from Ravanna, not Ram.
My uncle is a mastodon.
There are traces of white people in my saliva.
3.7 billion years ago I swirled in hydrogen dust,
dreaming of a planet overgrown with lingams and yonis.
More recently, say 60,000 B.C.
I walked on hairy paws across a land bridge
joining Sweden to Botswana.
I am the bastard of the sun and moon.
I can no longer hide my heritage of raindrops and cougar scat.
I am made of your grandmother's tears.
I am the brother who sold you, and marched you to the sea.
I am the merchant from Savannah, and the cargo of blackness.
I am the chain.
Admit it, you have wings, vast and golden,
like mine, like mine.
You have sweat, dark and salty,
like mine, like mine.
You have secrets silently singing in your blood,
like mine, like mine.
Don't pretend that earth is not one family.

Tiferet

Don't pretend we never hung from the same branch.
Don't pretend we don't ripen on each other's breath.
Don't pretend we didn't come here to forgive.

POETRY

Broken Future

Nicholas Samaras

How to fix what hasn't come yet?
Start with the anguish of the present.
Refuse to participate in what drags us
further down. Assemble the splinters
and rebuild a tree, a house, a space
to inhabit calmness and forgiveness.
Console what grieves and regrets.
Take coloured shards of a kaleidoscope
and reassemble a better picture, to break
the present and reset the bone.
To regenerate enough hope to live on.
To build a better home and move back in.

NONFICTION

Creative Collisions - Poetry as a Transformative Act

William O'Daly

The Meditation

From where do poems come? How do they grow—without and within?
What's the poet's role in the receiving and the making? Regardless of how one
responds to these ancient questions, poets spend years preparing heart, mind, and
spirit to compose the inner voice. They witness and speak out as their voice evolves
from other voices, from inner and outer processes and perpetual change. They commit to a lifetime of learning how to transfigure the steeple and the street, the cosmos
and the river, the fallen petals and the joy.

Seeking sources of vitality, poets and other dreamers— singers, dancers,
translators, visual artists, linguistic anthropologists, buffalo seekers—reach back to
the stories painted on cave walls; the symbols, customs, and memories ritually etched
in the collective imagination; the songs performed around the common fire. To this
day, Native American tribes perform their ceremonies and celebrate their traditions
around the ritual fire. Some preserve the old stories by originating from their spoken
language a written one. College and community writing workshops, another form
of community, can be helpful, depending on how a poet relates to them and learns.
The pedagogical thread encourages study of the lasting works, of prosody and poetics—of literature.

Artists in all genres, as lifelong learners, seek to discover and rediscover
themselves in the cultural landscape of which they are a part, of which they are an
expression. The more they explore the possibilities, the more unfathomable it all
becomes. As they become themselves, all that surrounds them becomes itself. Along
the way, we grapple with beliefs, theories, manifestos, invention and deconstruction,
edicts claiming how and even on what subject poetry should and should not be written. How poetry should not be written. How it should be.

But the poet's journey is of the kind any explorer, intent on observing
and creating rather than plundering and converting, might embark on. The poet
walks the plaza and the playa, grows imagination and intuition, an emotional and
intellectual life, and in the daily practice calibrates the internal compass. The poet

draws from the spirit of dream and of physics; the poem forms before the words. In twilight, the poem's substance is shaped by the practice, by how the poet dreams and perceives and breathes, even as, from the first beginning, the poem creates its own being. Poets witness how the poem shapes their relationships to themselves and to others, to the physical and the spiritual worlds. Discovering that web, they sing it, work within it. In the making, the poem costs everything and nothing.

In their singular worlds, poets speak of writing as taking dictation. In his book *Common as Air*, Lewis Hyde relates that the Hindu mathematician Srinivasa Ramanujan "believed that his family deity, the goddess Namagiri, visited him in dreams to write mathematical equations on his tongue." The same experience is shared by musicians and other artists and is amplified by those who translate poetry from another tongue. Poet-translators listen, intuit, think and feel in another language, in another history and culture. For a spell, they share in the perceptions of the poets whose works reach across borders, mountains, deserts, and oceans. They sharpen their eye and ear. In a sustained translation practice, they teach themselves their own language.

Why anyone writes, how anyone hears a poem and receives it, what impels a poet to commit to the art form—the answer is subject to personal and evolutionary forces. Whatever their fleeting or lasting form, answers arrive intimately, at some latitude and longitude, in their time. We experience them as unspeakable, as speakable only within a culture.

What good is poetry to the self or the other? Pablo Neruda's description of his poetics, of his roles as translator and reader, is of the essence. "Each and every one of my verses has chosen to take its place as a tangible object, each and every one of my poems has claimed to be a useful working instrument, each and every one of my songs has aspired to serve as a sign in space for the meeting between paths which cross one another, or as a piece of stone or wood on which someone, some others, those who follow after, will be able to carve the new signs."[1] Bradford Morrow, in the preface to his interview with poet, translator, essayist, and social critic Kenneth Rexroth, describes that American master's bearing: "What was so honorable about Rexroth was that, like any person who rises into true and genuine greatness,…he stood for what he loved and took a strong, active stance against what he believed was contrary to human dignity and the spiritual transcendence of the natural world."

Those artistic qualities and social positions, almost as much as Neruda's and Rexroth's works, have inspired many to emulate their commitment to the art form, to its communities, to the propagation of poetry and even making the world a better place. But no one ever accomplishes this by walking in the shoes of another. Every

---

[1] From *Toward the Splendid City*, by Pablo Neruda. Farrar, Straus & Giroux, 1974.

poet, writer or translator—any true artist—travels his or her own road, not only to prepare but to be open to inspiration and be filled with the voices of others.

Inspiration comes from the dry well or from light-years away, from the subway or the wave, and sometimes, when we pay attention, from close by—whether with a loved one gazing from the emerald hills upon the Florence of Dante and the Medici; or sharing with a friend on a clear, high desert night the moon lily; or sitting alone with a book and a hunger before the winter fire. Whatever the case, I take comfort in Antonio Porchia's words: "They will say that you are on the wrong road, if it is your own."[2]

Poetry is born of a commitment to living consciously, to succeeding and failing, discovering and reclaiming, and giving in a committed way. Poetry invites our dreams—and the dreams of others—to speak with us.

*   *   *

The Journey

My friend and I turn off Interstate 80 east of Reno, take State Route 442 a short distance to SR 447, and head north toward Surprise Valley. This evening we'll attend a reception launching an inaugural event to celebrate convergences among landforms, flora and fauna, the natural sciences and generative processes. We'll gather with friends and meet others who share a passion for the always becoming that is life, for the poetry.

As we pass through the arid, nearly treeless subbasin of the Great Basin, and despite knowing the deep blue will soon materialize, Pyramid Lake's sparkle comes as a revelation. It's the lake's southeast arm, not far from where the Truckee River empties High Sierra snowmelt into that sudden and salty waterbody. We catch sight of the iconic mounds along the shore, which my friend says are generations of crystalline tufa formed underwater in prehistoric times.

We rise and pass from that sunny subbasin to a rainswept one, between the brush-covered red clay hills bordering the playa. We steer our rented Prius along the bottom of what, 20,000 years earlier, was vast Lake Lahontan. Pyramid and one other lake are scant remnants.

Between conversations and speculations about what we're seeing, on the ground and in the air—a peregrine falcon, a Cooper's hawk, western scrub jays, Canada geese, a single snowy egret—I'm staring out the passenger window. I'm watching for metaphor, now feathered, where new expression might perch and call out and return to build its nest. I'm missing how tuned in I've been to rhythm and

[2] From *Voices*, by Antonio Porchia, translated by W.S. Merwin. Copper Canyon Press, 2003.

tone, how connected I've felt to unseen rivers and bridges, to destination as it develops on the page. We wind up and down the desert, climb another pass and descend into the next subbasin. Craggy formations and the dry sandy whiteness of the playa bring back the first stanza of Thomas McGrath's poem, "A Coal Fire in Winter":

Something old and tyrannical burning there.
(Not like a wood fire which is only
The end of a summer, or a life)
But something of darkness: heat
From the time before there was fire.
And I have come here
To warm that blackness into forms of light,
To set free a captive prince
From the sunken kingdom of the father coal.

We pass an exposed town beating back the desert, a town sunken and hanging on. Metaphor courses in this otherworldly, starkly beautiful landscape. The black hills to the west expand and contract with the morning light, while each day they lose some immeasurable part of themselves to time. Their breathing guides, moves us to listen to what's far away and what's nearby, to listen for the poem which appears first as rhythm, with a pulse and illusionary ease. Such a poem is what Neruda called a "rose of energy," one that grows in the imagination and transforms what came before.

The second and final stanza of McGrath's poem offers that same sense of renewal.

A warming company of the cold-blooded—
These carbon serpents of bituminous gardens,
These inflammable tunnels of dead song from the black pit,
This sparkling end of the great beasts, these blazing
Stone flowers diamond fire incandescent fruit.
And out of all that death, now,
At midnight, my love and I are riding
Down the old high roads of inexhaustible light.

The poet and his love warm with the ceaseless light of all that came before, pass the long night in the flaring, their union made sacred by the passage. They live forever in the light glancing off their bodies. The past thrives in those constel-lated forms of energy—in their ceaseless journey—in the dancer's muscle, the poet's cadence, the painter's dream.

As source and instrument, the poet transforms experience much as the jazz musician does the spirit when playing the tenor sax and much as the sax does the spirit when shaping the breath. The poet hears the undertones breathe *life* into something out of *nothing*, out of *everything*, out of what they *don't know*. Or maybe sometimes out of what, with mixed results, they know. The ancients, navigating the Arabian Sea or plowing the plains of central China, believed the earth was flat. What is self-evident is not necessarily accurate. What may be evident to the self can be ut-terly false.

Poets say they *receive* their best poems. In my experience, everything about the writing, and later the recalling of the process that brought such a poem into being, feels like being given the rhythms and the words—sensing or even hearing them without knowing their full measure, scope, or destination. This ineffable gift has long engendered fealty and gratitude in the poet, but to what or whom? Homer asks the Muses to sing the hero's failings. Catullus depicts as eternal the books given to the poet by the Muses. Dante equates the Muses with genius, and Shakespeare praises them as embodiment of invention. Whatever the myth or metaphor—in this era of the corporatization and commoditization of culture and self, of "nonpo-litical" poems and the exalted one, and, as Gary Snyder puts it, "the weirdness of television"—the belief that the poem is received acknowledges that the poet plays an integral role. But not as originator or font, not as one or zero. The poet and the work are diminished when the poet is, in the words of critic and translator John Felstiner, *ego*centric, not *eco*centric. That's because the poet belongs, as a transformative force, to the contiguous and continuous ecological and kinetic processes of the art form.

I think of belonging, as my friend and I pass silently through the motion-less town of Gerlach, gatekeeper of the Black Rock Desert and home of the Burning Man festival. Like any poet might, this town appears isolated but is fundamental to the shape of the human world, even more so when tens of thousands arrive to spend a few days in "tribal" communities, to receive and to give, to renew and be renewed, to just be there. An astronomical exchange occurs in that dust-blown region, where now there's nothing but the teeming life of the desert, silent, hidden. We motor past the unseen names of gold seekers carved in the rocks and the thrumming of spring water below.

The convergence of self-concealing life cools the fires and the echoes of Burning Man. It recalls the high school physics class I barely passed and the legend-ary skepticism of my teacher, Father Tobin. That oblate priest taught us that energy can be neither created nor destroyed; it can only be transformed from one class into another. For everyone's sake, I resisted the temptation to ask, "Even by God?"

With a glance heavenward and a nanosecond of stillness, Father Tobin gave a nod to Albert Einstein with the insight that matter is energy. Energy takes the form of matter and is conserved as matter; matter contains *potential energy*, which exists in constantly varying proportion to the matter's *kinetic energy* when the matter is subject to a physical change or set in motion. Unfortunately, now that I get it, it's decades too late to retake the final exam.

I've since come to see that poetry is subject to the same natural laws. The poem is language in motion, set and kept in motion by forces beyond the poet's control. As a college freshman, I followed Rainer Maria Rilke's advice to go within myself to discover whether I needed to voice *in poetry* my inner life. Does poetry gyrate in me; is it an urgency and a necessity? I felt poetry in the way Father Tobin lectured about "the catalyst," a stimulus to change that makes things happen without itself diminishing or changing at its core. Most days, yes, poetry did; other days, it did not, not that I could feel. That's when I thought I understood relativity, even as I foolishly tried to know place and motion at the same time.

What restored my belief in the calling, was the poetics of Charles Olson. In "Projective Verse," Olson circumnavigates the poem as a "high energy-construct and, at all points, an energy-discharge." The poet prepares the "composition by field," attentive and ready to receive, to reel in, to gather up; to avail of natural gifts and acquired skill; to be present and shape language in genuine and changing proportions. I began to know in my bones—when the poem arrives and is performed aloud for others, or when it's read silently—energy is exchanged, a cycle of give and take. When the poem bridges languages and cultures, the energy of the original transmigrates. It lives in the poem in translation, not as a clone but a new poem. Potential and kinetic energies coexist in the original and the new poem, in an intimate relationship that forever binds their separate lives.

If all matter is a product of change, poetry is born of exhaustion. As land artist Robert Smithson observes, poetry is "a dying language" and a language that never dies. It occurs when matter gives way and energy acts upon it; a consequence of the sum of natural laws, it becomes something else. Although this flies in the face of how people often talk about the creative act, the evidence is all around and inside us. The astonishing formations of ignimbrite in the Hayes range, bordering Surprise Valley to the east, were formed by the hot suspension of particles and gases. Those particles and gases flowed from a volcano, driven by a much greater density than that of the surrounding atmosphere.

Tiferet

When we climb, physically and in our imaginations, a sedimentary formation that resulted from a pyroclastic flow, the formation becomes for us the austere glass- and crystal-encrusted stone perch of the goddess Ignimbrite. Then, that poorly sorted result of primeval "fiery rock dust cloud"[3] is transformed into poetry by those participating in the conference.

Why *goddess Ignimbrite*? Because the formation sings of incomprehensible transmigration, of the fertile remnants of creation and destruction. We revere, are in awe of, the energies converging further back in time than anyone can comprehend. This energy is present and in a form that animates us. "Once an inner gift has been realized," writes Lewis Hyde, "it may be passed along, communicated to the audience. And sometimes this embodied gift—the work—can reproduce the gifted state in the audience that receives it."[4]

Nothing brings this home more than a night visit to the playa. Several of us drive across the dry, sandy lake bottom. We turn off the headlights and pile out of the car, into the darkness. No moon, no ambient light. Just dim points along the western edge of the valley, whose light in no way obscures our view of Cassiopeia, Orion, Scorpio, the Big Dipper, and nearby Venus. The Milky Way streams across the black sky with a consuming brilliance I've seen only twice before: once when I camped at age fourteen in the Mojave Desert, and then during the predawn hours when I sat alone, at the northeastern rim of the volcanic crater Rano Raraku on Easter Island.

I swore I could hear the neutron stars, the pulsars—incredibly dense, rapidly spinning remains of burned-out super giants light-years beyond our sight—speaking in radio waves. When the core of a supergiant star collapses with the exhaustion of its fuels, material distant from the center moves closer. Like a spinning ice skater accelerates by pulling her arms into her body, the star spins faster and faster.

In the same neighborhood, supernovas. Farther out, quasars emitting unfathomable light swirl around black holes. They speed up and draw closer, release energies beyond measure. They live billions of years later in our retinas and photographs, in our minds and hearts and words, even as untold eons ago they ceased to exist as matter.

Much closer, all around us and within me, I could feel the faint tremor of the meteorites and the comets that over four billion years ago collided with Earth, the cataclysm depositing minerals and water needed to sustain life. I felt remarkably at home among all that momentum and death, gravity the unifying force and

---

[3] New Zealand geologist Patrick Marshall derived the Latin-based term *ignimbrite* from "fiery rock dust cloud."

[4] From *The Gift*, by Lewis Hyde, Vintage, 1983.

exhaustion proof of gravity's existence.

Life is the liberation of energy, as is poetry; it demolishes preexisting relationships. Its *gravitas* constellates memories, perceptions, emotions, intuitions, and ideas in new relationships—from which derive the poem's musical shape and cadence, the quality and the nature of its perception. Gravity brings the poem into being and eventually destroys it. This brief poem, inspired by "What the Water Knows," by the late Sam Hamill, is one shard of that process:

> What the heart reveals
> can only be given away.
>
> What the feet acquire
> is emptiness of mind.
>
> What the mind knows
> only water can grasp.
>
> What the spirit seeks
> is everywhere.

We're evidence of poetry born of exhaustion; the act of lovemaking and our life cycle obtain in the same way. Our poems and poems in translation do so, too, in our DNA. We go on writing from a shift in perspective or some other change of life. The poem breaks at the edge of laughter or of tears, when the work is "closer to death than to philosophy, closer to pain than to intelligence, closer to blood than to ink."[5] All poetry authentic and true—the goddess Ignimbrite or Lake Lahontan, the brazen brown hills flanking us or the desert populated by music and fire—survives as energy and, in turn, makes our survival vital.

> If each day falls
> inside each night,
> there exists a well
> where clarity is imprisoned.
>
> We must sit on the rim
> of the well of darkness

---

[5] As Federico García Lorca described Pablo Neruda (translated by Steven F. White).

and fish for fallen light
with patience.[6]

    We are the answer to the poem's miraculous relations, as is the poem to ours. As witness of our existence, neither the poem nor the poet is alone. Intellection about how poems should be written trails in the wake of the daily power of poetry, impelling us to sustain the art not so much as an act of will but as a condition of being human. Poet and poem collide with what is, who they are, their strengths and their weaknesses, their hidden songs and their vulnerability. Poetry sustains us, revealing what it is *to be*.

---

[6] From *The Sea and the Bells*, by Pablo Neruda, translated by William O'Daly. Copper Canyon Press, 1988, 2002.

TIFERET WRITING CONTEST WINNER
NONFICTION

Gods for Other Lives

Laura Marshall

There was snot on my white oxford sleeve and my mother's fingernails were digging into my forearm. Everyone at St. Christopher was staring as I howled-- elderly women clasping crystal rosaries, men kneeling at the rear pews with missalettes, and some of my second-grade classmates, who were also there to make their first confession before First Communion next week.

I had refused to participate in the sessions we lined up for after Mass at school. I loathed interactions with male strangers. I like to think this is a quality I would admire in my own hypothetical seven-year-old daughter, but to my mother it was a grave sin and a deep embarrassment. She was a devout Catholic, and New Orleans is a city where Catholicism is a cornerstone of local culture, the dominant educational system, and practically a governing body. Believing in God and/or Jesus was almost beside the point. At seven, I understood religion to be a reason to receive Christmas presents, which is also more or less what I understand it to be as an adult. Mass inspired certain ritualistic practices for me, but not the ones my mother or teachers intended: it was my designated time to write stories that might best be characterized as *Ninja Turtles* fanfiction in a pink Hello Kitty notebook.

I wasn't even sure what to confess. In religion classes, seven-year-old sins had been suggested to us: talking back to your parents, hitting your brother. But even with a script, the matter of talking to a stranger, of being alone, was frightening, too intimate, and I didn't see how telling someone else about a sin could change the past.

After I tried to storm off for a fourth time, Father Ken emerged from the rear of the church, chuckling and walking in our direction. His hands were outstretched, and then on me, and I screamed in wake-the-dead horror as he picked me up by the underarms and said *come on, now, it's all right* and carried my flailing body all the way to the altar and placed me in a chair before a different priest.

I sat in silence, tears soaking the front of my blouse, as the other priest recited the Act of Contrition on my behalf and volunteered sins for me. Then I ran, bright colors of stained glass blurring around me. My mother caught up to me and sighed. "I'm sorry," she whispered when she caught up to me. "I didn't know -- I didn't know he was going to pick you up."

Tiferet

For the rest of my childhood Sundays, I'd scream and beg to be left at home when my mother woke us up for Mass. I only tolerated going for the Christmas season, up until the day in early January when our discarded tree would be picked up for the coastal restoration effort: a festive wall for a doomed land.

*

I willingly entered a church again only once, for another funeral in my final year of high school. I was fifteen when Kyle was diagnosed with leukemia, a progressed level that was discussed in percentages rather than in treatment options.

Kyle and I did musicals at a community theatre together in the summers, and we were often partnered together for dance numbers. The town he lived in was in a more rural stretch of land near oil refineries and chemical plants that has now been nicknamed "Cancer Alley" for its uncommonly high cancer incidence rate. On the interstate, you soar past earth and swamp until you see an oil refinery in the distance, rising above the coastline. Imagine how Oz looks from the beginning of the Yellow Brick Road, but as if it was host to a recently contained fire: a green, glowing horizon interrupted by a smoky sigh.

The two years following his diagnosis went like this: transplant, remission, more cancer, chemo, remission, more cancer, four months to live. Four months turned into three weeks and then all I remember is receiving a terrible phone call and my father knocking on my bedroom door one morning: *Baby, what's wrong?* And then, after some utterance from me, just these words through the crack at the bottom of the door: *Jesus Christ.*

*

Five months after his diagnosis, Katrina was careening toward the coast. We evacuated that morning and drove for six hours, then eight hours, then ten hours. No vacancies. We finally found a Red Cross shelter that had been established inside a Baptist church's community center, where each family sat in its own rectangular section of carpet marked off with masking tape.

There was no TV, no power, no news as the roads closed, only intermittent radio. We didn't know how Bad it was until several days later when we got into a hotel room. Nothing on a screen seems real: if you get close enough to the TV it dissolves down into the little red, blue, and green squares that constitute the projected images. I elected not to believe it. I had to see it first.

It would be weeks before the roads back to the city would be accessible, so we went to Houston, where I enrolled in a public school. I was one of only three or four displaced "Katrina kids" in a student body of over three thousand students, and so was asked questions like: *Did you lose your house? Does everyone flash for beads at Mardi Gras? Why do you even bother living below sea level?*

Few students even asked me my name. There was no reality to my experience to them: they watched me like a television show they could click through as soon as the action slowed down. I was an aberration; they were normal kids. I didn't see myself in them at all. I didn't see myself anywhere, not even in my own reflection as I dropped ten pounds in a month.

But I knew my family had no right to complain, so I didn't. Dozens of my friends had lost everything. That was the phrasing everyone always used: you either Lost Everything or you hadn't. And we hadn't. Where does your experience go when it is, maybe too literally, a drop in the bucket? The present seemed already in the past, like our lives split into two entities we had to live in concurrently. Not Before Katrina and After Katrina, but two parallel rivers running toward the same murky gulf.

*

The last time I saw Kyle he was trapped beneath a web of tubes, covered in liver spots, his arms splayed to either side of his body. My level of denial about the situation had increased until my mother drove me to the hospital between classes and rehearsal one afternoon with the insistence: *you need to see Kyle right now*. When you are raised in a religion of miracles, all you can assume is that, in a life-or-death crisis, a miracle is what you are due. I had to believe in the miracle because to believe Otherwise would result in-- in what? Some kind of cosmic collapse?

We walked through the hospital and I went into Kyle's private room, alone, watching his unconscious body pulse with the rhythm of the ventilator and whatever other artifice was keeping him alive. After a moment, a middle-aged doctor in wire-rimmed glasses and blue scrubs entered. He had a mask on, but tugged it down to his chin to talk to me. Here was the thing about the children's hospital: people at least knew not to talk to you like you were a child. There was no mention of heaven, no dumbing things down. Everyone knew that you knew things you weren't supposed to know yet and treated you accordingly.

I kept my eyes on Kyle as the doctor spoke to me in numbers and levels to explain the infinitesimal ways in which Kyle was doing better today than he was yesterday. I said nothing, but nodded, grateful to be spoken *to* and not *at*. In my peripheral vision, I saw the doctor open his arms toward me. I collapsed into them, howled: I now believed Otherwise.

*

They say the Louisiana coastline loses a football field of land every one hundred seconds. It seems impossible, fantastical, that if it were true the whole country would be underwater. It is certainly a rate beyond what Christmas trees can fix.

The news surrounding the rebuilding effort of New Orleans became controversial, sometimes hostile. I knew, logically, that there was an argument to be made against living in New Orleans and the area surrounding it; I knew that the coastline receded every year; and by 2005, I knew that the planet was overheating and that all of its sea levels were rising. But now there were scientists and journalists and engineers advocating for its abandonment.

I tried to imagine a fully recreated New Orleans further north. A replicated streetcar line, French Quarter, City Park, St. Louis Cathedral. All the oak trees cut out of the ground and rerooted. But the map of my brain hit the Mississippi delta, hit the tiny Cajun town my grandmother had left to come to the city. Even if a chop-and-drop fantasy could become a reality, it would be devoid of its history, the narrative that gave it music with equal parts pain and joy, the cuisine steeped in doing the best with what you have and letting nothing go waste. If that story has nowhere to go, I thought, maybe we're all better off drowning.

In 2010, the Deepwater Horizon oil spill newly scars the water, the city, its food source. I come home from college for my twenty-first birthday, and as we watch the pelicans suffocate in brown muck on television, my grandmother says in her rich Cajun accent: *Dey sent someone to de moon. Why can't dey clean up de erl spill?* She passes away two months later, and her funeral constitutes my final entry into a church.

*

Two months before Kyle died, I was drained from all the work of a compressed senior year of high school and its aggressive attempt at normalcy. Things were not going as planned, despite my engagement in the requisite senior year activities. I had no idea what I wanted to do after graduation except go to New York: I was at the top of my class and no closer to choosing a college than I was to climbing Everest.

One day in October, just after we had finished midterms, I had no assignments or deadlines to attend to during our hour designated for independent study. The instructor policing this hour was a young teacher named Ms. M., really not much older than we were at about 25, who hated me.

I rested my head on my desk and Ms. M barked, "Marshall. Do something, read, anything. No sleeping." I tried to read a book, but when my head found itself in my folded arms and she barked again: "Marshall. Wake up. What's wrong with you?" Her voice felt like stitches being ripped out from an unhealed wound.

"I'm just so tired," I said. "I don't have anything to do. I just want to sleep. Can I just sleep?" I was crying in a real way, that awful gasping and snorting way. She and my classmates stared at me with round O mouths. I asked to go to the restroom and stayed there for the remainder of the period. What was wrong with me?

She didn't care. No one did, because no one knew what was going on. Kyle wasn't a student at my school. I could have told her, but maybe I didn't want to. Maybe I wanted a certain suffering to myself. People are protective of nothing as much as their own pain. I didn't know how or where to honor an experience I had that no one else understood, or even objectively knew. If the stories that make you who you are are the ones no one knows, do they still make a sound?

*

Kyle's funeral was celebratory, though, not somber. Everyone wore his favorite color, lime green, and the packed church was filled with songs from musicals he loved or had performed in with his friends. We gathered in the parish hall afterwards to share memories and stories and photographs and more songs. A slideshow on a projector showed Kyle and our friends in costumes for various musicals, Kyle and I at the last homecoming dance we went to, Kyle as a baby, Kyle with his twin brother, Kyle in his first car.

A few months later I dreamed him back to me: we were dancing the choreography we had done as partners in *The Music Man*. It had been years since we'd done the production, but I woke up and knew the choreography was exactly the same. Muscle memory, rehearsal, 5-6-7-8: a religion, a prayer, a rite in the absence of others.

*

The rebuild, rebirth, re-New Orleans movement hit with the subtlety of the storm itself. The roads had barely reopened and everyone was in contest to prove their loyalty, their commitment, their local authenticity. New Orleans was like a religion that had the best of intentions but had gone wrong: a city known for being friendly and welcoming now in cultural civil war. It was not the city I grew up with and not the one I wanted to be around, even though I knew this was what it looked like when people were just trying to keep themselves alive.

I still felt guilty when I left for New York in 2007. But I arrived to a sudden, cold freshness, to people who knew nothing about me and cared even less.

It was two years post-Katrina, which for residents of the Gulf coast region was functionally two minutes: you could still smell the rot of it like you can smell saltwater from the beach. I didn't understand until then that it had been more or less forgotten by the rest of the country, and few people I met asked me about it. Most assumed that I moved as a direct result of Katrina, and filled in any other circumstantial blanks for themselves. *Why do you bother living below sea level?*

I was wildly alone and I loved it: making up who I was as I went. I didn't mind when people made assumptions, projecting stories onto the blank slate that I was. But just when I was becoming the person I'd be for the rest of my life, the dam breached and the oil spilled and one sunny afternoon in my senior year of college a man broke into my apartment and raped me and strangled me and I would never find out who that person would have been.

*

Imagine a book with all of the words scratched out with a knife. Emptiness, void, complete and utter godlessness. For the next three years or so I was nothing but surface.

Marshall, what's wrong with you?

My two settings were working or panicking, so I did the only things I knew how. I finished college the next semester and continued to go to my customer service job with my same perky *HowMayIHelpYou* voice. People still yelled at me over their ticket purchases or their own mistakes. Now every time I speak to an unhappy customer service representative I wonder if they were raped the week before.

It's one of the things no one ever knows. Or understands, if they do. There were only three people I knew who did understand: a girl crying in church in second grade, a girl mourning a friend that no one knew was dying, and a girl trying to answer the question *Why do you even bother living near sea level?* I came across this haiku but could never find the author: *I can't abandon/the person I used to be/so I carry her.*

*

New Orleans came back to life like grass pushing up through soil: as long as there was sun and oxygen it would always return. But I stayed in New York, with its own resurrection pushing a new tower into the sky.

When I met more people in New York and told them I was from New Orleans, I came to know the slow nod of locals, of those who had lived in the city before September 11th. It was a nod of recognition, an acknowledgement of-- despite the vast differences-- shared experience. A home fractured beyond recognition; a city amidst ungoverned chaos; already-disastrous situations becoming stuff of cosmic proportions with one final, forceful breach of a damaged barrier; the fact of being suspended in space and time for so long that you don't know what outcome you fear the most. Bodies frozen in space, falling or floating, stories with no known endings. Maybe this is why I needed to move to New York: maybe the only way I could see my own experience was through someone else's, from a distance of miles and years.

*

They say it takes seven years for your body to fully refresh itself, for all old cells to be new once again. Seven years to create a new body, a cocoon-like reemergence, regeneration, renewal. Rebuilding. I wonder if this is, in some realm of existence, true, and if it so for places as it is for bodies, for the dead as it is for the living, for invisible histories as it is for the visible. I wonder if anything is lost the renewal process, like dust or ash or snakeskin, and if we get to choose what we keep from past iterations, or if some things are just washed away and forgotten. I wonder if the thing is still what it was before it was destroyed or disappeared or transformed. I don't know that. But here is what I do know: I kneel before the girls I carry with me, and I light candles for them so they can see in the dark.

TIFERET WRITING CONTEST WINNER
POETRY

Outside Grenoble

Jennifer Barber

What I remember most
is a confusion of bells,
the sheep like woolen slipknots
over the tufted grass.

The din of dogs
warned us off
as if we'd come to abscond
with a lamb or two in our arms.

Hundreds of feet below,
the city lay in a haze
of cars, buses, and heat.

Where the trail
went under the trees,
we heard the cuckoos' cries,
contrapuntal, invisible.

Let me pour it all once more
into the cup of my ear:
the bells, the cuckoos' calls
back and forth overhead.

However far, let me keep
all of it now among
my gathering flock of things.

TIFERET WRITING CONTEST WINNER
FICTION

What's Left

Mary Grimm

"Wouldn't you like to have your lunch?" Carol says to me.

"What's it like out there?" I say, and she says how nice it is, how warm, a little breeze. She's coaxing me, and I don't like to be coaxed. "No, I don't think so," I say, and then say it again when she says the birds are singing out there and the flowers look so nice. As if it was Disneyland out there.

I can't see it so well anymore, but I know what it looks like, for I did it all, except we had the lawn planted, I remember how terrible it looked, the house in a sea of yellow dirt, hard clay, like a rock when it was dry. But every bush is mine, all the trees, the day lilies along the bottom edge, next to Jensen's house. Their cat used to hide in there, I'd have to chase him out. The hostas along the foundation, the wild hyacinths by the front door. The sweet gum tree—it's gone now, wind damage. The Japanese maple. I can still see the Japanese maple pretty well, even from in here—a cloud of red, its leaves are like lace. There aren't a lot of flowers—a rose from my mother's old house, a bleeding heart by the side door. The lawn is restful. You look at it and your mind quiets down. The lawn and the trees. I can hear someone hammering.

"What is that noise?" I ask, and Carol says she doesn't know.

"Only half a sandwich," I say to her, and she sings it back to me as if we were in a choir.

She's not the worst of them, the home health aides. I don't want her here, don't want any of them, but she's not the worst. The worst was tall and skinny and smelled like an old closet. She liked to watch the soap operas, which I can't abide. She'd put them on when I went to lie down, I could hear the murmuring of their voices, all those people having each other's babies. My daughter Elaine thinks I'm naïve, but I know what goes on, it's not that I can't deal with what people do with one another. Elaine thinks I'm afraid of the word itself—sex—and it's true that I don't throw it around like some do. I was a loving wife to James. Where does she think she came from, for heaven's sake? Someone had to do something to someone.

Another of them wanted to talk about God all the time, wanted to pray with me. Linda her name was, or Lindy. She was young, as young as my granddaughter would be if Elaine had had children. Young and pretty, but she wouldn't shut up about God, something that should be for private and in church. And then another one that pinched me. I showed Elaine the bruise and she looked like she might cry, I could see the way her mouth turned down even with my bad eyes.

"Look at that," I told her, "that's what it's doing to me, having these people in my house." I thought that she might send them all away then, but she didn't.

"I have a life," she said to me, crying it out in the voice I recognized from all those years ago, when she was a teenager and we fought all the time. It was like a knife cutting me, for her to say that. I have a life and you don't. Your life is over. Can't work, can't cook, can't go out, can't walk. Her life against mine, what's left of it. It cut me and I had a picture in my head of that empty space I see sometimes, a hole, my life falling out of it.

I had a chance then to say to her what I know, what she ought to know, but I held back, I couldn't say it, what is coming, what the end of all this will be. I don't know why. If I don't say it, it won't come true? like when we wished on a star? Close your eyes and wish, I remember my sister Polly saying that, I couldn't have been more than four years old. I could see the star like a pinprick in the dark, the light from the kitchen pouring out behind us where we stood in the back of the house, the barn dark against the sky. Don't tell, she said, or it won't come true. What did I wish for? a doll, maybe. A doll with real hair and a china face. And now, do I want it to come true or not?

I have a life, she said, and I guess she does—books and school and students. Men sometimes, one after another. Why can't she get married again? Can't, she says, twice is enough, and she's right there, I guess. Who knows what kind of rats she's wasting herself on, but a woman can't be choosy after thirty-five. You have your chance when you're young and you have to find a good one and hold on to him. I got married the year I was thirty-five, but I wasn't on the shelf. Too much going on to get married—the Depression, the war. James didn't mind waiting. Elaine might as well be an old maid for all the good her looks did her—no children, no husband— one divorced, one dead.

"Here you are," Carol says, sing-song like she does. "Some nice tomato soup and half a grilled cheese." I let her give me an arm up and I go across the room, inching, stiffer than usual. My chair, the pillow adjusted, I sit into it, almost falling at the last minute. Sandwich could be hotter, but I don't say anything. She has some applesauce in a little bowl, and a cookie. "Just one won't hurt," she always says about the cookie, which I'm not supposed to have. She brings them with her to this cook-ieless house and can't bear not to share them. Not homemade cookies, she's nothing of a cook. Storebought, but sweet and crisp. I hold it ahead of me like a star, the end of lunch. My calcium pill is on the counter next to the mug, but Carol pretends she doesn't see me put it in the garbage. She puts on the weather so I can hear it for myself.

Did you get that?" she says. "A high of 85." Eighty-five, I say, it doesn't feel that hot to me. You're just skin and bone, she says, you don't feel the heat. She laughs and says how she's better off in the winter, with all her padding. I don't want to think about winter, and I tell her so—the very idea makes my bones feel cold, how they tighten and stiffen in the winter, I almost start to shiver, even with hot soup in my mouth. Half the soup, almost all the sandwich, all the applesauce. Carol can't brew a good cup of coffee, but at least it's hot. The hot coffee in my mouth to take away the thought of winter which is like a white empty space, the wind howling. I can still hear the hammering. Maybe someone is building a house back behind the woods.

A sip of coffee, a bite of cookie, the sandwich kind with a cream filling. I could eat another, and Carol would give it to me if I asked, but I don't for I know my numbers will go up. Elaine doesn't think so, but I can manage my diet, I've been doing it for years. I don't need her or the doctor telling me any different.

Carol is taking my plate and mug away, starting the dishes. She's sloppy about it, always splashes water on the floor. She never dries anything, just leaves it in the dish rack. But I'm not in charge anymore. Everybody's made that pretty clear. She's talking, talking, her grandchildren, her church group, her husband's prostate which I certainly don't want to hear about. You don't have to listen to her, she doesn't care. Her voice is fat, like she is, cushiony, you can rest on it. One bite of cookie left, a sip of coffee. Time to go to the bathroom, coffee in one end and out the other.

"You go on," Carol says, as if I'm leaving the party early. "I'll have a little sit-down while you're napping."

"I don't like the word nap," I tell her, "I'm not a baby," and she agrees, but she'll call it napping again tomorrow and the day after.

"What's your daughter doing today?" she asks me while I'm getting up. She always asks about Elaine as if she were some kind of film star. A college professor, she'll say, isn't that wonderful. Nothing wonderful about it, I say to her, but of course there is, first in her family to go to college. A teacher, what I always wanted her to be, and what she finally came around to after going all around the barnyard.

"I don't know what Elaine's doing," I say to her. "She doesn't tell me."

"Probably has to meet with her students," she says, and I say, "It's summer, for heaven's sake," because my back is hurting me, and I am dreading going to the bathroom, all the lowering down, the awkwardness of the walker, the mess. I never really feel clean anymore.

Tiferet

"Some of them teach in the summer, don't they?"

"Not Elaine," I say, and it hurts to say this, for if she's not teaching why can't she be here? why does Carol have to be here if it's summer?

Once I am in bed, my knees drawn up to ease by back, my Kleenex and rosary where I can reach, I sigh. My eyes are wet, not real tears, just tiredness. I'm always tired. My window, the shade pulled down. The room is dim although I can see the brightness of the sun outside, an outline around the shade. James's bed, neat as a pin. I couldn't bear for it to be stripped, couldn't bear it, even though he'll never sleep there again. I made it up myself for years, once a week, changed the sheets, put fresh ones on, plumped the pillow, smoothed the blanket, turned it down just the way he liked it. Elaine does it now, I'll give her that. I never had to say it to her, say do your father's bed. Sometimes I imagine I see him sitting there like he used to, he'd sit and take off his socks, we'd say a few words. We always had twin beds, it's healthier for sleeping. He'd take my hand sometimes before we fell asleep.

In the dim of the room, I turn my head toward his bed, even though it makes my neck hurt, and of course he's not there, no shadow of him, no ghost. I don't want him to be, not really. He's out of this, gone from pain and sickness, I don't want him back. Or if I do, it's only when I'm really low, when I can't be myself for a while. If one of us has to die first, who do you want it to be? I asked him a long time ago, a game we were playing. We'll both die together, he said. What, in a car accident? I said. I wouldn't like that, too noisy, too messy. A soft car accident, he said. No really, I said, who first? He wouldn't answer me, but I was sure he'd wait so he could be here for me. I think I rested on that, counted on it. But here I am, stranded. He's gone. Just me and Elaine. As a little girl, I never thought she'd turn the face to me that she has. What would your father say, I want to ask her, if he could see your face now.

Sleep in the afternoon is different from at night. It's harder to go there, to go into it. Afternoon sleep is light, you can feel the daylight on the other side of your eyelids. At night sometimes I can still sink into the dark, a real forgetting. Sometimes I can dream that I am not old. But in the afternoon, if I have dreams they are sticky, annoying, the sounds of real life poke into them and make them ugly and broken. I can hear Carol's footsteps as she moves around the house. I don't like to think of her looking at my things, picking them up, leaving her fingermarks on them. She says she dusts, but it's nosiness, that's all. Looking in drawers, fingering the books on the shelf, taking the pictures down off the walls to squint at them. I can hear the wind outside, it comes into a dream about Elaine, about her husband, the one I didn't like, or the one I liked least, something about his hat, about a stain on the hat, the wind blowing through it, the leaves rustling against the window. He takes his hat and throws it into a lake, and from across the lake which has appeared in my backyard, I can hear the hammering, and I rise almost all the way out of sleep, saying so loud that I'm sure Carol will come, what is it? what are they building?

NONFICTION

William Morris: Beyond the Borders of Disappointment

Adele Kenny

William Morris was born on March 24, 1834. The eldest of nine children and the son of a wealthy London stockbroker, he lived with his parents and siblings in a large country house near Epping Forest until he was thirteen years old. Later stating that he was born out of his time, he spent his childhood absorbed in medieval lore.

While a student at Oxford's Exeter College, Morris met Edward Coley Burne-Jones, a young artist who was mentored by Dante Gabriel Rossetti, one of the Pre-Raphaelite Brotherhood's founders. Young, idealistic, and gifted, the Brotherhood denounced idealized Renaissance art and rejected Victorian materialism and pretension. Committed to revolution against the strictures of Royal Academy art, they pioneered the path of British artists toward greater individuality, realistic forms, and attention to detail and color. Morris's personal philosophy and long-time interest in the Middle Ages found sympathetic values in Pre-Raphaelite beliefs. Although the original Brotherhood dissolved in 1853, disciples and a second wave of Pre-Raphaelites embraced what is now known as Aesthetic Pre-Raphaelitism, which, in turn, led to the Arts and Crafts Movement and modern functional design. Along with a shared interest in medievalism and Arthurian legend, Burne-Jones and Morris would become part of that second wave; and, in 1856, they became roommates.

In 1858 Morris wrote "The Defense of Guinevere," a long poem dedicated to Rossetti. As fate would have it, the poem was oddly prophetic of Morris's marriage and his wife's later liaison with Rossetti. Jane Burden was modeling for Rossetti when he introduced her to William Morris. Rossetti was already deeply infatuated with her, despite his long courtship and marriage to Elizabeth Siddal. The daughter of a stableman and an illiterate laundress, Jane came from a less than desirable background; and as a poorly educated artists' model, her marital prospects were badly lit. That notwithstanding, Morris married Jane in 1859 when Morris was twenty-five and Jane was eighteen. Morris was overweight, unkempt, and had an untamed temper. On the flip side, he was financially secure and socially well connected—in short, through marriage, William provided Jane with easy conveyance into the upper echelons of polite society. By her own admission, she was not in love with him.

Although Morris once planned to pursue a career in architecture, he discovered a stronger inclination toward design. In 1861, he established the London-based firm of Morris, Marshall, Faulkner, and Co. in partnership with Burne-Jones, Rossetti, Ford Madox Brown, Philip Webb, Charles Faulkner, and P.P. Marshall. Dedicated to "organic" fine art workmanship, they produced and supervised production of furniture, wallpapers, murals, tapestries, stained glass, metal works, tiles, and embroidery.

Morris's work was revolutionary in an era when mass production resulted in lower standards of design and quality. Rejecting the elaborate embellishments of Victorian decoration, he focused on nature and the uncomplicated but rich gothic devices that found favor during the Victorian Gothic Revival. Morris believed that the decorative arts were an expression of natural beauty and that a home should only contain items that were both decorative and useful. In Morris's words, "have nothing in your houses that you do not know to be useful, or believe to be beautiful."

The first years of Morris and Jane's marriage were seemingly successful and two daughters, Jenny and May, were born in 1861 and 1862. Sadly, Jenny suffered from epilepsy, and was consigned to live in the long shadow of an illness that carried with it considerable stigma during the Victorian Era (when the sociology of the condition was underscored by fear and repulsion). Things were also troubled in the Rossetti household. In 1862, shortly after the birth of a stillborn daughter, Rossetti's wife died of a laudanum overdose, a presumed suicide. Disenchantment and tragedy set the stage for Dante Rossetti and Jane Morris.

While Morris worked at his art and business, his wife began a passionate affair with Rossetti, who shared the lease and lived with Morris and Jane at their Kelmscott Manor home. Morris was well aware of his wife's infidelity and his friend's betrayal. That Rossetti was obsessed with Jane is undeniable. That Jane married Morris as the only means of escaping her lower class life is also a given. The living arrangement was unconventional at best and destined to fail.

During the early 1870s, Morris visited Iceland, which became a spiritual holy land for him, spurred him to involvement in British Marx-based Socialism, and inspired a series of poems and translations of Icelandic sagas. In 1871, while Morris was in Iceland, Jane was left at Kelmscott with Rossetti. Morris, while not condoning his wife and his friend's affair, did not take any action against either of them and, apparently, "allowed" them a degree of freedom. Divorce was not an option for several reasons. Clearly Morris adored his wife and would do nothing to hurt her. He also valued his friendship with Rossetti. There was no such thing as mutual divorce in Victorian England and, as a divorcee, Jane would have lost Jenny and May as well as her reputation as a respectable woman. Obviously, though, for those close to Morris and his wife, the arrangement at Kelmscott was well beyond socially acceptable limits of propriety.

In a nineteenth century "Camelot," Morris was cast as Arthur with Jane as Guinevere and Rossetti as Lancelot. Morris seemed to have resigned himself to a failed marriage and his wife's affair with Rossetti; however, in 1874, Morris declined to renew the shared Kelmscott lease. Rossetti moved out, and Morris later relocated with his family to the smaller Kelmscott House. During 1875-76, Rossetti took a cottage in Sussex where Jane stayed with him. She was, however, disturbed by his paranoia and his addiction to chloral and whiskey and, in the end, she returned to her husband.

A year before Jane returned, Morris bought out his partners, and the firm became Morris & Co. As Morris experimented to recover old weaving and dying techniques that had been displaced by the Industrial Revolution, the firm's textiles became popular with the wealthy upper classes, and in 1881 the company was hired to redecorate the throne room and reception rooms at St. James's Palace. Although Jane returned to Morris and continued to work with him, she remained in contact with Rossetti through correspondence and infrequent visits. She saw him for the last time in 1881. Rossetti died on April 9, 1882, after which Jane began another affair with minor poet Wilfrid Scawen Blunt. Whether it can be attributed to the vagaries of human relationships or to Morris's stoic character, he remained with Jane despite her continued infidelities.

In December of 1884, Morris founded the Socialist League, giving speeches and talks on street corners, in working men's clubs, and in lecture halls throughout England and Scotland, as well as in Ireland where he supported Irish nationalism. An1885 manifesto published by the League featured cover art by Morris. A year later, the Black Monday riots of February 1886 resulted in amplified political repression against left-wing agitators and, in July, Morris was arrested and fined for public obstruction while preaching socialism on the streets.

In 1887, Morris designed special wallpaper for Balmoral, Queen Victoria's residence in Scotland. However, Morris's commitment to artistry and his efforts to employ medieval techniques to create simple and beautiful products for common folk was a cost-intensive enterprise affordable primarily to the elite. This undoubtedly buttressed Morris's involvement in promoting social reform.

In 1892, Morris was elected master of the Art Workers' Guild; he was also asked to become England's Poet Laureate, an honor that he declined. By then, his personal life with Jane was increasingly unhappy and, although he remained close to his daughters (especially May who shared his artistic nature), his health was poor. Perhaps still under the spell of the Pre-Raphaelites' attenuated romantic ideals, Morris found consolation in writing prose fantasy romances during the last few years of his life.

The work of Morris & Co. continued during Morris's final years. Production included various stained glass windows designed by Burne-Jones and six narrative tapestry panels depicting the quest for the Holy Grail.

Although Morris left few paintings, his furniture, wallpapers, innovations in textile manufacture, superb stained glass, and typeface designs became world-known. His Kelmscott Press, founded in 1891, led Walter Crane to call Morris "the first to approach the craft of practical printing from the point of view of the artist," and the *Kelmscott Chaucer*, designed in the Medieval illuminated manuscript style that Morris hoped to revive, has been described as the most beautiful volume produced since the Renaissance. Morris's political and nonfiction works are still widely read and collected, and his utopian prose fantasy *The Wood beyond the World* (1894) greatly influenced the fantasy and science fiction genre.

When William Morris died of tuberculosis on October 3, 1896, his doctor gave the cause of death as "... being William Morris and having done more work than most ten men." One of Victorian England's most noteworthy cultural figures, Morris was best recognized during his lifetime as a poet but is known today as the father of the Arts and Crafts Movement. Most importantly, he was a generous and big-hearted man who learned to live life beyond the borders of disappointment. He wrote of his place in history, "The past is not dead, it is living in us, and will be alive in the future which we are now helping to make."

NONFICTION

Constellating World Peace, One Family at a Time

Jamy Faust, M.A. & Peter Faust, M.Ac.

There are many paths to peace. Together as a couple, we have been on an astonishing journey through our family lineages that has left us yearning for more. More peace for ourselves and those we love, and more peace for everyone on the planet. Dismantling the internal borders that we erect to our family and loved ones is an essential aspect on any path of peace.

To borrow the words of the Dalai Lama,
One person can influence their family, one family can influence another, then another, then ten, one hundred, one thousand more, and the whole of humanity will benefit.

We have come to appreciate that humanity's movement towards peace really begins one person at a time, one family at a time. Most of us desire peace for ourselves, our species, and our planet. But our collective progression towards peace has to begin with each of us—in our willingness to first embrace the spirits of our mothers and fathers to gain understanding and compassion.

Think of it this way: each of us is a continuation of our respective family lineage, of all that has occurred in the lives of our ancestors. Many of our internal conflicts were handed down to us in the form of unconscious beliefs. To begin a path that leads to peace, we need to look no further than the circumstances of our own birth for clues to those conflicts and even in choices made before birth. Of course, our struggles as adults also have roots in our developmental years.

As a wife-and-husband team who have facilitated Family Constellations for hundreds of people seeking to heal their familial relationships, we have noticed that most of those who come to us understand that lasting peace requires moving beyond talk, analysis, and rehashing family stories. They seem to know intuitively that real peace requires a more daring journey into their family lineage, to uncover what some call the Family Soul. Over time, we've come to understand that Family Constellations can offer more than emotional or psychological healing. They can also provide fresh insight into the unconscious (or Soul) agreements made with our parents, siblings, and ancestors. Moreover, it allows us to see why particular events and experiences may have occurred in our lives. This awareness, once we integrate it, inevitably sheds new light on our attachment to pain and suffering caused by separation. The healthy boundaries we once created to support individuation can often turn into intractable borders. Natural boundaries become rigid and immovable borders build over time.

You must be wondering, What are Family Constellations?

Family Constellation is not a new form of psychotherapy, a trendy "New Age" spiritual practice, or some other panacea for everything that ails you. It is an innovative method that helps to reveal hidden dynamics in family systems or other relationships, so that conflicts can be acknowledged truthfully and healed. The practice of Family Constellations is a way to relax the borders that separate us from spiritual understanding, happiness and a sense of peace in our soul.

We first learned about Constellations through the teachings and philosophy of Bert Hellinger (12.16.25 - 9.19.19), a German-born psychotherapist, analyst, author, and former Catholic priest who, until his recent death, contined to teach packed seminars worldwide. Other practitioners have also made significant contributions to the field of family systems theory, but Hellinger is widely regarded as one of its leading pioneers. Some have suggested that the original inspiration for his philosophy came from the sixteen years he spent working alongside the Zulu in South Africa, while he was still a priest. Central to his philosophy is the importance of honoring one's ancestors.

Our own experiences and trainings with Bert Hellinger, both in the US and Europe, opened each of us to a new path in our personal healing, and ultimately, to helping and teaching others how to heal and find peace as well. Hellinger showed us ways to enter the Constellation process through the frame of the Family Soul, which enabled us, in turn, to expand our work into a larger collective field.

Imagine your family—extending through several generations—as a constellation. Each family member, alive and deceased, known and unknown, represents a star, so to speak. The relationships among these various stars in your lineage have created their own unique patterns and dynamics. You are who you are (and I am who I am), in part, as a consequence of these ancestral dynamics.

Tiferet

In your personal healing and movement towards peace, no amount of reading about Family Constellation theory or practice can serve as a substitute for your own first-hand experience of a "live" Constellation, led by a well-trained facilitator. The facilitator helps gently guide the process from beginning to end. In most instances, there are three additional roles in a Constellation: the client is the person who has chosen to work on a particular issue; the representative(s), as the name implies, represent family members or other important people in the client's life; and meta-representatives sometimes stand in for phenomena such as an illness, one's family religion or ancestral homeland, and even war or other forms of violence and trauma.

Exploring our family lineage in a Constellation provides the opportunity to uncover secrets and hidden truths, and to investigate aspects of our lineage that may be unexplained or even lost. A Constellation allows us to examine, sense and explore energetically the borders between conflict and peace. Boundaries and borders are the crucial crossing points that bind us together as a family. When we begin to look at these things with open eyes, hearts and minds, we're able to let go of attachments that no longer serve our lives. A Constellation helps to remove the borders of separation, so the consciousness of connection can flow more easily between loved ones. Through a Constellation we can also experience the new strength that comes from a more conscious and meaningful connection to our family lineage.

Consider for a moment one of our personal stories. This one involves Peter and his father:

My father contracted polio when he was six months old. The shadow of his physical limitations—what was called a 'handicap' in the language of the time—hung over all aspects of our family life, like an ever-present companion in our household. As a boy I felt the loss of not having a father who could throw a ball or teach me how to ride a bicycle.

In a Constellation, standing across from representatives for my father and for his polio, I instantly became aware of the judgments I held for my father. Acknowledging that I had seen him as somehow less than a father brought waves of shame that made me drop to my knees. I saw before me the two-halved man: one side under-developed, skin loose, small muscles, bones visible, the effects of a body ravaged by polio; the other side a normal, strong man's body. Half was not good enough to get a good-paying job in those days, or to throw a ball with his son. I had judged my father the way the world saw him, as less-

than, not good enough, as not man enough.

The Constellation brought me into a space where I could see beyond his physical body. Acknowledging him for who he really was, not the way I wished he had been, led me into the realm of acceptance. It helped me to release the judgments and the shame and allow me to finally see him for the teachings and love he had given me through his disease.

I remembered his extreme patience and his methodical way of explaining things that he could not physically do himself. I remembered how together we could accomplish what he couldn't do alone. I saw how he passed on to me his love of reading, writing, and learning.

I instantly understood, by being in silence and looking deeply into the eyes of the representative for my father, that he had transformed his shame into dignity. My father had lived every day of his life since infancy with his handicap. Out of that life he had developed a pride and dignity that can only be learned through an aversion.
In that moment the internal image, the border I had created in my heart and mind, separating me from my father was completely transformed. I no longer pitied or felt sorry for him. Instead I was overcome with feelings of pride and gratitude towards my father. I wept with appreciation for him.

This is but one example of how a Family Constellation can open up a completely different perception of our life situations and relationships. If we're willing to simply travel into the depths of our consciousness, start the process of dismantling our internal borders, change and healing can begin at the level of personal consciousness, then ripple into our family consciousness, and eventually affect the collective consciousness of humanity.

Lao Tzu, the ancient Chinese philosopher, said it best:
If there is to be peace in the world,
There must be peace in the nations.
If there is to be peace in the nations,
There must be peace in the cities.
If there is to be peace in the cities,
There must be peace between neighbors.
If there is to be peace between neighbors,
There must be peace in the home.
If there is to be peace in the home,
There must be peace in the heart.

As growing numbers of us seek a path of becoming peacemakers and peacekeepers, may all our efforts work together to heal the consciousness of humankind everywhere on the planet.

POETRY

Grandma

Catherine Doty

Mischief made her lift her arms and turn
with such a look of wonder on her face
that I was not afraid to see the flames
licking along both sleeves of her flannel robe,
but stepped back, as one does from an act
of God, the better to take in her glittering
pale green eyes, her pirate's nose, the few
yellow teeth in her little open mouth
as my mother, her own mouth open
in a scream, rushed up behind her to yank
off the blazing robe and dance on its burning,
and Grandma, naked, jubilant, winked at me
while the kettle shrieked its way to boiling dry,
and sent me from some far hilltop in her far world
a sneak peek at what it was likely I'd become:
wild-eyed and crazy and blazing like a six-gun,
nothing at all to be met with shame or fear.
So this is for her, who now has long been ash,
another small poem the last word of which is *oh*.

POETRY

Stop Time

Doug Anderson

I had to get out of the car.
I thought of my first love.
The trees were covered
with ice crystals and the sun
was coming through them.
I thought of you and how
little we knew of anything.
But we had everything.
A sudden wind and the crystals
make the sound of a beaded curtain
with a ghost passing through.

POETRY

Apple 2.0

Elizabeth Cohen

let us get this right, finally, and stop blaming the woman
she was smart and curious she had her own ideas

the birds and ants and bees were understanding
they had been feeding on the sweetness for years

the sky and the tree understood
even the apple, the apple itself, knew it was ok

I am an apple, the apple thought
I am not sin

afterwards, all the animals, the sky, the ants, the bees,
the leaves, the trees, the rain

even the serpent, watched
as she was expelled with him from the garden

and then they became immigrants
and learned to feel shame

POETRY

While Out Jogging I Come Upon the Graveyard of the Insane, Bryce Hospital, Tuscaloosa, Alabama

Jack Stewart

Suddenly among the fallen leaves
Flat stones, some numbered,
Most empty enough to line
A plaza or circle a fountain.
No sense of when
The troubles started, the numbing
Of synapses for love or belief.

All you can see through the autumn-thinned trees
Are the trunks of more trees.
I have no opinion
On what treatments should have been tried,
Just a wish someone had paid for names,
Even initials,
Anything that would say these bright,
Fragile souls had once been known
By someone,
Even if it wasn't themselves.

POETRY

Questions

Jude Rittenhouse

1

Who are we? Really?
Are we more like trees, fulfilling dreams
of acorns and seeds, or are we sea's
children: forever transforming from mist
to fog to cloud to rain to river or lake
until our homecoming—our re-union?

2

Wind's vehemence kept me
awake last night: he screeched
through high limbs and hills,
hurled rain by fists-full. I wondered:
Has our oldest oak sunk anchors deep
enough? Will maples, chestnuts, cedars
and oaks whisper encouragement
to each other through their roots, survive
this nor'easter's tantrum? Let me be
honest: fear, not wind, prevented me
from dreams. Fear
and his cryptic sister chanted their couplet
of questions: Am I safe? What is safety?

3

What waits beyond memory
and what if we could bear living
without answers? Our questions

Tiferet

strung between birches like prayer flags.
Offerings.
Might we then believe
childless old women? Their wild hair
streaming like moonlight on a river:
enchantment's dance. Revelations
unending.

POETRY

Fused

Judith A. Christian

I was not brought to this sallow light
to see, and as in every case
of creation, the ant cresting the dome

of its hill, for example,
sand scratches the eyes
or vision is dulled by clouds

floating on the viscous fluid
that moistens the globe.
And even fused

into a solid form by the sudden
stun of insight or sun
what I become is only

glass, a window, keeping out
keeping in, until someone
comes along to open me

or I lower my head to my knees
and crawl outside to peer
into the tunnel, my pupil

an inch from the ground.
What a long way they go,
the ants. What a long way to go

to see the end of oneself,
to see the beginning
to break glass

to shatter every you
every me.

POETRY

One

Judith Harris

So many years ago,
my mother sits in the kitchen
trying to teach me
the numbers of our address,

in case I'm ever lost,
her face flushed
as I keep forgetting the 1
in "10618," and insisting on "1068"

as the place where we lived.
Now, on the anniversary
of her death, I am rebuilding
our red brick house from memory,

the ringed stump of an oak
bereft of its trunk,
a lone shoe, or stray mitten,

our shadows linked on the stairs,
as I sat there then,
my lips mimicking hers,

reciting "1068" over and over—
as if reciting Kaddish,
trying but failing to bring back
the missing one.

POETRY

Annunciation

Judith Harris

Here, the Virgin is seen
tending her garden.

How it blooms, and blooms
in a succession of whites, followed by
schemes of magenta,

the blossoms contracting,
then immediately open,
succulent fruits ripening on the vines.

How many angels would be summoned
to persuade her of the miracle
planted within her;
the story already foretold?

Look, how the gold brushstrokes
shine through her lapis blue draperies,

sending the masters back to their tasks
to practice their craft
hour by hour,

illuminating one world
with the careful light of the other.

POETRY

An Immigrant Mother Talks to Herself at the Mexican Border Detention Center in Tornillo, Texas

Laura Boss

And though I thought crossing the border
    was saving my three year old son
    from a future like his older fourteen year
    old brother killed by M13 gang members for
    resisting to join
And though I thought I'd save my five year old
    daughter from the dangers of rape in puberty
    like her cousin from those same
    gang members
And though I imagined a life in a small Texas town with
    a decent school system where they can dream of being
    a teacher or even president(though I hope not like this
    one who wants a wall and yesterday rips my children from me)
But tonight sleepless in this detention cell, I imagine the cries of my *ninos*
    not understanding why we are separated, the younger one missing
    his pacifier (maybe just as much or more than me)
And I think our lives are a smashed piñata that is empty.

POETRY

I Used to Listen to the Saddest Love Song

Maria Giura

I used to listen to the saddest love song—
Bonnie Raitt's "I Can't Make You Love Me"—
especially in the months before breaking up
with my first real boyfriend.
"Why such a sad song?" he asked innocently,
when he heard it on my voicemail.
"I like it," I said, lying.
He wasn't my soul mate, my forever,
the direction my life was supposed to go.
 "You Can't Make Me Love You"
would've been more accurate,
but I was grateful for this small mercy
as I tried preparing him and me,
but especially me,
for the long sadness that was to come.

A Review of
Saint Peter and the Goldfinch
Poems by Jack Ridl

BY MARK HILLRINGHOUSE

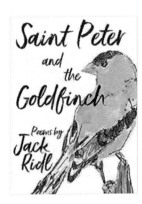

SAINT PETER AND THE GOLDFINCH
Poems by Jack Ridl
Wayne State UP, 2019
112 Pages
$16.99 Paperback and eBook
ISBN: 9780814346457
eISBN: 9780814346464
To order: https://smile.amazon.com/Saint-Peter-Goldfinch-Michigan-Writers/dp/0814346456/ref=sr_1_1?crid=22UYL6Y4WVRWY&keywords=saint+peter+and+the+goldfinch&qid=1565096977&s=gateway&sprefix=saint+Peter+and+the+%2Caps%2C124&sr=8-1sr=8-1

When writing about Michigan poets, one thinks of Roethke, and his last book, *The Far Field*. Jack Ridl, a Michigan poet, writes his own "Far Field" in this collection, his latest from Wayne State UP, titled *Saint Peter and the Goldfinch*, but the journey Ridl takes the reader leads into morning sunlight, not afternoon darkness, and into the arms of mindful awareness of things that matter.

Ridl is a poet of the long, gray Michigan winters, but his winters blossom in intense, green springs. The local landscape is his palette. He is like Monet in his Giverny. Reading him you will learn the names of two dozen wild birds and dozens of flowering trees, plants and shrubs. The voice inside these poems is one of solitary contemplation, of a man looking outside cataloging the day's discoveries.

He's a master of the tightly crafted enjambed couplet and triplet stanza. The collection is divided into four separate chapters or sections. The first section titled "The Train Home" sets the tone and lays down the tracks for the poems to come. I love the ease with which Ridl tugs at the reader as in the preface poem "Likely" in this first section that begins: "Most days come/ along like a child/ kicking a stone"/ And I love the way his poems leave the reader with a mystery as in the following poem, "It Was last Night, I think" that ends, "I have jars filled/with words my/ father left behind./

There are other voices in Ridl's poems and echoes of other poets, William Carlos Williams included. In Ridl's poem "Wondering What It Was Like" in his first section, Ridl, like Williams, raises objects to the level of conscious awareness as they appear to the mind's eye as in the following lines:

…Something in that house

Calmed every word. Something lay calm
on everything: the broom leaning against
the sink, the pot on the stove, the tables,

cups, books; peace even seemed to lie within
the rugs. His mother called us to the window
and said, "look!" There was a male cardinal,

black chin against its violent red, sitting
on a snow-covered branch. And then I saw
the tractor, snow piled on its metal seat,

and then the wind-sculpted snow drifts.

And like Roethke in a faint echo of "North American Sequence" Ridl's metaphoric structure creates a comparative world through metonymy and synecdoche as in Ridl's poem titled, "American Suite for a Lost Daughter" that begins:

I am the last greylag on the left side of the V.

I am the amen in the prayer you never say.

I can bring some stones to you, to the place
you left as a child, the place where the wolves

Tiferet

came to drink and watch you. They watched
you through eyes set deep in the land.

.....

The poem goes on to share the speaker's paternal loss of a loved child and the
existential longing and anomie amid unanswered questions from the celestial
universe that turn into prayers.

One of my favorite poems from the first part of Ridl's book is the poem titled,
"While the Dog Sleeps." It is a poem about domestic peace and quietude in the
quiet comfort of meditative silence in the contemplation of passing time gathered in
the image of a sleeping dog. The poem ends with these stanzas:

> "tomorrow" is a strange word, "now"
> even stranger. "Yesterday" makes sense,
> but not much of it is true. Our dog still
>
> keeps sleep. I imagine him dreaming
> la dolce far niente. When asked
> if I miss what I did for forty years
>
> I like to say, "That never existed."
> Now here on the porch I take in the light
> crossing the last leaves doing their slow
>
> dance in the breeze, watch the chickadees
> at the feeder, once in a while glance at
> the sundial we set in the shade of the redbud.

Ridl's speaker's past haunts these poems, poems for his daughter, for his brother dead
at childbirth, for his mother and father, for his aunt, for dead poets. Some of the
lines reveal his speaker's guilt and self-hate and self-punishment. In the poem, "The
Train Home" a kid escapes the cruelty of his household in the basement hoping to
transcend self-punishment.

Ridl's poems are his replica of the world he rejoices in and of the world he feels
distance from as he returns to his domestic corner of his universe to peaceful dogs

to growing his garden to feeding his chirping birds. Whether it is in removing the names of dead friends from the rolodex in the poem "Turning to the Psalter" or to getting rejection slips in the mail in the poem, "Self-Pity as an Ars Poetica," Ridl always reaffirms the speaker's existential dilemmas.

I would advise readers to pick up this volume of over eighty poems in the morning and read from the beginning, read a few poems in the waking morning sunlight in the way consciousness returns after sleep while still steeped in dream. And things begin to reappear one by one so that you marvel over each one's existence. Ridl's poem, "The Man Who Decided to See" announces the second section of the book of meditative excursions into that realm.

The poem, "Dailiness" in the second section, is about conquering time. It is about a man who has his whole day in front of him and how he will plan the day ahead after breakfast going from the deep past to the present to the near future:

.....

> what lay ahead: he would feed the fish
> in his little pond, cut back what had died
> in the flower bed, get pumpernickel bread
>
> and orange marmalade, then the mail, maybe
> stop at Jane's Depot and buy some new
> warm socks. And he needed to decide
>
> what book to read next. And what
> to have tomorrow for breakfast when
> the angels would be back around 7:30.

The angels Ridl refers to are literal angels, the children playing in the snow. The title poem, "Saint Peter and the Goldfinch" is the next poem, and it is filled with the literal things of his speaker's world:

.....

> ...He liked thinking
> he had nested. He liked thinking everything

here could be taken away. He had cosmos,
impatiens—no perennial until bloom
and loss became ritual, sacred. There was

a breeze. There was the tea. And then there wass
a goldfinch, just one, at the thistle feeder, its startle
of yellow and black seamless within its feathers.

Peter watched as it took the seed, sat above him.
He watched as the bird flew to the feeder, flew back
to the same branch. Saint Peter and the goldfinch

here in the day's beginning. He could not bow
his head. He knew joy's coupled sorrow. He knew
that this was time. He knew what the earth knew.

After the title poem, the speaker seems free to go to other places—an agenda-less journey of a wandering soul, the poems in the section that follow in a middle chapter, take the form of suites, of numbered stanzas in a series of meditative odes. It is a more lyrical body of work titled, "The Long Married" and which unfolds in poems that mirror the stages of life of a speaker who inhabits the still center of his spinning world.

In Ridl's poems there's a longing for what lies underground as in the poem "The Inevitable Sorrow of Potatoes". It is a longing for what goes unseen and for what passes beneath our knowing. And like D. H. Lawrence's "Blue Gentians" Ridl's sorrow takes us deep into the earth. But the darkness is relieved by the juxtaposition of the poem "Key West Suite" which follows the winter darkness with bone-white, bleached-coral sunlight.

You can take the poet out of Michigan, but Michigan never leaves the poet's interior. There's a Wallace Stevens "snow man" melting in the Florida sun in this poem, as in the last section, section VI, subtitled "Blue Sky over the Bight" that begins:

Sometimes when we stand in the loss
of it all, surrounded by what we will never

be, the sky seems to be just fine. It's blue.
It's many shades of blue. And it's there

And will be when we join the landscape
of the invisible. Clouds cross, none ever

the same. And that's when we realize again
that there actually is no sky, just another

anonymous unknown we are sure to see.

...

In the final section of Ridl's book—Waiting for the Astronomer—there are poems about Chinese ink drawings, meditations on photographs, poems about what professors say about their students, and there are poems about meditation, and about what it means to pray and how to endure the endless cycle of dharma. These are poems written to comfort the soul. The title poem of this last section speaks to that notion:

.....

... An astronomer
can measure the negative space

between each star, the absence
of light within the extravagance
of a galaxy's quickstep and

disappearance. Over the earth's
wobble, eternity is a calculation.
Instead I write my name

in the dust along the windowsill,
the star's lost light falling across
the vase of flowers on the kitchen table.

I know that I will go back to these poems and read them over again the way I go back and read poems that matter to me because they are poems written out of

Tiferet

necessity. This collection is the work of a poet who wants you to share what he has learned about what it means to rejoice in the everyday.

FICTION

Entry

Allen Kesten

He's held on an outlying hill surrounded by the sea. The cinder block hut has only one window, small and square. It's above his head, out of reach. There's no furniture to step up on, so he can't look out. He must sit on the bare floor to type. His knees ache from sitting cross-legged before the aqua typewriter, the floating rows of black keys. The hut's metal door is always locked.

There's a radio, but it has no batteries, no cord. Was it placed there with the intent to torment him? At night, when the wind howls or airplanes buzz the hilltop, he thinks he hears music coming from the radio, the ghosts of songs he used to listen to back home.

What sounds like the same military truck that brought him here returns once or twice a week. Supplies are passed through an access portal at the bottom of the door.

One morning, after the usual delivery, a crying child is shoved through the opening. Then the portal is quickly shut and locked again. He reaches over the child and bangs on the door. The smell of the ocean rises off the girl, salt and seaweed.

He tries to go about his usual routine of sorting the delivery. Food, toiletries, housekeeping supplies. The child cries where he left her, limbs folded in. Her sobs are like spider silk sent out to snare him.

⁓

The girl can walk but sometimes reverts to crawling, though he thinks her too old for it. She can't or won't talk. She takes care of her own toileting, and he's grateful for that. He's careful not to approach her too suddenly. When he sweeps the floor, the broom gives her wide berth. She seems like the abused street cats he remembers from his boyhood: guarded, suspicious, easily provoked to howling for long periods. He feels overwhelmed and resentful when she cries. What of the silence that allowed him to work on his application?

⁓

His body a raft, he arrived hopeful on the nation's shore. Despite being immediately detained and kept in isolation, he tried to hold onto his vision of the future. He still imagined the friends he would make, the neighbors he would greet walking to work in the morning, the nods and smiles as his new life flowered. He even allowed himself to dream of a companion, a hand to clasp. Yet anxiety, the madness of not knowing, was a snake constricting his heart.

On the fifth day of being held, the hut's larder nearly empty, the first delivery of supplies arrived. There at the bottom of the box was the instruction booklet for *I-589, Application For Asylum and for Withholding Of Removal.* He spent hours studying the booklet and making notes. Then he sat before the typewriter, its presence at last making sense, and rolled in a sheet of paper. He felt a facility with the machine return. As a student, he had earned money typing papers for classmates, fingers fleet until two were broken.

He followed the template laid out in the booklet. Part I. NAME. COUNTRY OF BIRTH. OTHER NAMES YOU HAVE USED. The steel typebars rose like legs marching as his fingers tapped.

Part II. DESCRIBE YOUR CIRCUMSTANCES. It embarrassed him to write about himself at length when there were thousands like him back home, still trapped, voiceless, forgotten. In the end, he pretended his handwritten notes were the work of someone else, and he merely tasked with organizing and typing them.

As he worked through the night, he layered his petition with deference to the Immigration Judge that would review his case. "Your wisdom, caution, and foresight are the keen protectors of your country's way of life. I submit to your judgment."

The application, folded in exact thirds and placed inside an envelope imprinted with the Department of Security seal, waited by the door until the next delivery. After the supplies were pushed through, a beckoning hand appeared through the portal. First, he gave over a bag of his collected refuse. Then, before the portal closed, he handed out the envelope. The hand reappeared, gave a thumb's up, and then withdrew.

As he listened to the truck drive away, he felt exhilarated at the thought that his case would be considered, moved forward.

However, that night he regretted nearly everything he had written, from the tone of his supplication to the punctuation.

In the morning, he composed a letter explaining his need to revise and replace his application. "My first, rushed attempt was beneath your consideration. Excitement overruled prudence. Please forgive my mistakes in the use of your language. I learned it as a boy in school from an inadequate teacher."

He reconsidered every word and phrase he had written, discarding many. He searched the instruction booklet for clues as to how to improve his chances. Finding few, he embellished on the obsequiousness from the first application, adding, "Sir, you and a hundred other judges could defile me and I would still love your country, your people." Humiliating himself with hyperbole was nothing compared to the suffering of the people back home who defied death each day.

A few days later, he handed off an envelope containing the letter and the revised application.

Then in its own delivery, he received a reply from an immigration clerk. "The Judge assigned to your case is a very busy man with many petitions to consider. There is no way to predict when he will adjudicate your status. Your request that the newly received application stand in place of the first is granted. If you deem it necessary to send additional revised applications, know that our office will accept each and dispose of the one before until your hearing is scheduled. Once your name appears on the Judge's docket, we will notify you. Only then will your application be read by his Honor. Concurrently, a desist order will be issued against further submissions of applications. As the grandson of immigrants, I am sensitive to your plight." Had he found a friend at the Department of Security?

The relief he felt that the revision had been accepted was soon eroded by gathering anxiety. That night he began to compose another revised application.

⁓

The girl begins to acclimate to life in the hut. While he types, she sits opposite him, her eyes wide with amusement at his exasperated sighs. Her head bobs with his rarer nods of satisfaction.

Sometimes, while he fixes their meals, he spies her tiny fingers creeping across the floor towards the typewriter. She pulls them back at the sight of his scowl. He won't allow her to touch the machine, for he fears she'll somehow damage it before he can produce one faultless application.

At night, she climbs under the mat the authorities finally thought to send and sleeps on the bare floor as if covered by a blanket.

⁓

As the weeks of solitary internment passed, he submitted more revised applications, each time almost certain that he had made the most persuasive case for himself and was done. One night, unable to sleep, it occurred to him that the standing offer to accept revisions might have been just a ploy to heighten his constant state of disquiet and self-doubt. He walked around the square of moonlight on the floor. "Or," he wondered, "was the intention to encourage more of my self-degradation? Do the Department clerks huddle together and read of my willingness to be exploited, abused? Are they aroused by it?" Still, he revised, typed, sent.

Tiferet

After he had dispatched seven applications, a photograph of the Secretary of the Department of Security was delivered with a directive to hang it on the wall. Tape was provided but proved useless on the raw concrete; the picture fluttered to the floor within hours. He placed the portrait beside the typewriter. He had hoped to see some capacity for mercy in the man's eyes or kindness in the set of his mouth. But he saw only disdain in the hard, angry face. Eventually he turned the picture over, finding it easier to write to the faceless Judge of his imagination; the magnanimous and unbiased man he hoped would review his case.

Sun bright in the window, he lifts the girl up so she can look out. He can't see her eyes and what might be reflected in them. It's then that he most regrets that she doesn't speak.

He thinks he should submit an *I-589* application for her, but is stymied at the start. Although he has asked her many times and in many ways, his hand sailing between his chest – *my name is* – and her shoulder, he still doesn't know even so much as her name.

One day, along with supplies and food, a paint box arrives, six bright, oval cakes of color and a thin brush. A label on the bottom credits a relief agency for the gift. He hoists the child to the window again and then sets her down with a few pieces of discarded paper from drafts he didn't send. Together they discover how to swish the brush in a cup of water and then moisten the paint. Maybe she'll show him what she's seen beyond the grey hut.

He notes the girl's presence in his next revision, but without clear purpose. "I care for a child placed with me. To the best of my ability, I try to teach her things." Then he adds, "Perhaps her paintings will please you." (He doesn't reveal that sometimes he has to pry the brush away as she rubs it violently over the paper, shredding her work. The brutality and persistence in her hand shocks him, her pain loosed by the color and the water.) The photograph of the Security Secretary is kept under the typewriter now, face down. He is tempted to give it to the girl as a canvas for her anger and frustration, but doesn't out of fear.

As the weeks pass, the child ingests only powdered milk and sleeps most of the time. There is still no notification of a date for his case, no reason to stop revising.

When the child's slumber is restless, he stops typing and places his thumb in the palm of her hand to reassure her of his presence, his watchfulness. Her fingers close around it like the petals of a flower at night. Sometimes she opens one eye. But surely she finds him lacking; he knows he's just skin over an empty armature compared to a mother's warmth and love, or a father's adoration and pride.

He has rewritten the story of his life so many times, read so many iterations, that the words are like tinkling pieces of colored glass, their connection to the sand from which they began all but lost.

Although he's slow to accept it, the girl is wasting away. He types a letter to the clerk. "I'm sheltered with a child who has fallen ill. Perhaps she could be moved to a hospital." He wonders if the letter will be read or just treated as another one of his revised petitions. Will it be left unopened, saved until the next envelope arrives, and then destroyed? Using the child's paints and brush, he writes "Urgent!" on the envelope in red and hopes this will gain someone's notice. When the truck comes, he bends his head to the access door as he hands out the letter and implores, "Please. The little girl needs a doctor." He vows not to write or send another application if there's a chance the girl can be saved by the letter. It must stand.

Two nights later, still waiting for help, he's roused by a change in the atmosphere inside the hut. He gets up from his mat to check on the girl. He discovers she has died in her sleep. Looking at her open hands, he thinks, "She'll never be reunited with her family in this world."

Everything in the room seems suspended in the air, and time resists its course. His tears are a wall of water he must swim against.

Eventually the fabric of the universe reweaves itself. He feels the concrete floor beneath his knees, sees the light of the rising sun glowing in the window. He rolls the child's body in her sleeping mat and says something like a prayer over her.

The next day, when he hears the truck approach, he waits with the body by the door. The pass-through is opened and a first aid kit drops to the floor. He wants to scream at the sight of it. Before the door can shut, he shoves his foot against it. Then he lifts the dead child from the floor and hands her out.

In the revision he submitted before the urgent letter, the girl's existence had been documented once more. "She's a lovely child in need of a home, a place to play, sunlight, a family."

Now he realizes that if he sends another application, one that omits any mention of the the girl, her life will be effaced. A second death. Still, he wonders if he should complicate the application that will ultimately be read by the Judge with pleas for a child now gone. After a day of mourning, he's back at the typewriter.

Tiferet

Month pass; he doesn't know how many. The hut's door is left unlocked now, and he can wander the hilltop whenever he likes. Is it a sign that he's been forgotten? Perhaps he's no longer considered a danger, just a nuisance. Being able to stare up at the stars in the night sky is some compensation.

When he hears the truck approaching, he opens the door and greets the man who brings supplies but no news. Although the man seems too old and diffident for the uniform he wears, he has a gun in a holster hanging from his belt.

One morning, he asks the old man if the child was properly buried. The man tilts his head to the bay and says, "After a fashion."

His hopes and aspirations have been cast off, refuse from an existence in stasis. He wonders why he keeps revising his application, except for the fact that he believes there's still a perfect one to be written, and this has become its own vocation.

He hands off another envelope. As he climbs into his truck, the old man mutters, "So many like you, suspended, feet prevented from really touching the ground." The truck turns around and heads down the hill.

Around the bay, he can see the hilltops poking through the fog, their cinderblock huts an affront to the blue sky above. And he imagines clasping hands with other detainees, a rebellion gathering above the mist.

He holds the metal can of powdered milk, untouched since the child's death. How many moments of gladness with her had he missed because of his obsessive typing? He hadn't marked the days she was with him, heeded each one. No, he was too caught up with revisions, paragraphs polished to dust while the pages of the instruction booklet came loose from the staples that bound them.

Sensing something new shuddering through his hands, he kneels over the typewriter.

He doesn't know where the pride he suddenly writes with comes from, yet it blooms, faint but familiar. He has never worn fatigues or a uniform. No medals have dangled from his chest or hung around his neck. He has never held or carried a gun. The wars prevented him from earning a diploma. Was pride fixed within him at birth and even more miraculously, sheltered all these years? He was loved, by his mother. He imagines her breath entering him now as if she were saving his life.

He types with determination, banishing all words that beg, stoop, and apologize. Instead, he uses words that declare, insist, and claim. He wants the paragraphs that describe his life to have the power and mass of islands risen from the ocean floor.

III. WE LIVE IN A TIME OF LIMITED RESOURCES. ASSURE THE STATE YOU WILL NOT BE A BURDEN. EXPLAIN. Although he responded with pages of self-effacement before, this time he writes only, "I will contribute to your nation, bringing dignity and purpose to any work I'm allowed to do." He thinks about his inattention to the fledgling girl. Had her family endowed her with pride, or had it been up to him to bestow it? When he raised her up in his arms to the window, did she gather her worth to him, to this world? Shaking his head he types, "My soul was diminished when I shielded myself from the needs and gifts of another. Is this to be your nation's fate?"

At the end of the application he adds, "There was a young child with me. She died neglected, in despair." He must ensure her life and death are documented in what he knows will be his final petition.

Folded in thirds and placed in an envelope, he leaves the finished application on the cement step outside the door, a stone to hold it down. He is done. It won't matter now when the desist order comes, for he has stopped himself.

Feeling exhausted, he lies on his mat. His eyes remain fixed on the typewriter. He hears the ghost of his tapping on the keys. After a time, he rises, lifts the typewriter from the floor, and carries it outside. His shadow is cast before him, the sun warm on his back. At the edge of the hilltop, he lets the typewriter drop. The machine clips the slope of the hill, dust and debris following its fall like the tail of comet.

A Review of
A Reminder of Hunger and Wings
by Jane Ebihara

BY ADELE KENNY

A REMINDER OF HUNGER AND WINGS
by Jane Ebihara
Finishing Line Press, 2019
31 Pages
$14.99 Paperback
ISBN: 978-1-63534-835-4
To order: https://smile.amazon.com/Reminder-Hunger-Wings-Jane-Ebihara/dp/1635348358/ref=sr_1_1?keywords=Jane+ebihara&qid=1565111630&s=gateway&sr=8-1

Jane Ebihara's poems in *A Reminder of Hunger and Wings* are those of a mature woman who has worked through loss and longing with resilience and determination. Her examined and realized life is deftly expressed through finely crafted language and richly layered imagery.

The collection opens with the poet's first memory.

> From "First Memory" (p. 1)
>
> she hears her mother call
> but stands
> still as stone
>
> her first memory
> this one
> of quiet rebellion

Throughout this collection, that quiet rebellion carries Ebihara through memories that bring back what she's lost *and* gained in coming to terms with heartache and in rebuilding her life.

She writes of her mother's death, of returning to a place that is no longer home, and the futility of grief for what cannot be retrieved:

From "The Day after You Died" (p. 4)

what strange familiarity
this place
where you no longer live
where I no longer live ...

I might slide off this road remembering
be found by locals
who'd say *she's a stranger here*
we'll have to see where she came from

it's late   too late   too late

Always moving with clear momentum and a sense of trajectory, Ebihara uses imagery drawn from nature to explore and situate what it means to be human:

From "Listening to a Distant Thunder" (p. 11)

... there have been simple signs
things out of place
          that groundhog in the tree
          the tree frog on the windowpane
          words that batter like moths

it hesitates now
this summer storm
teases   then falls quiet
still we know it stirs
know it will weigh us down with its magnitude
we know too much malice
will uproot us

storms are like that
          picking things up

> putting them down
> where they don't belong

Keenly observant of human frailty, Ebihara's work is an intimate narrative underscored by hope.

> From "Almost April" (p. 15)

> what's left of winter

> sullen dirty mounds of what was beauty
> misshapen stakes set to guide the plows
> dismissed carrots thrown to hungry deer
>> who roam
>>> slack-skinned and hopeful

> you and I
> still here
> watch snow that does not melt
> listen for birdsong
> we cannot hear
> just yet

These are poems of reckoning that pay attention to line and sound. Their sonic impression rests on competent application of such techniques as alliteration and assonance. Clever use of caesuras and enjambments (that equate to breath pauses and phrasal units) result in line breaks so specific that they don't require punctuation and allow silences the time they need.

Compressed and tight, no line or stanza becomes an attenuated thought. There is no superfluous language—nothing unnecessary—in these poems. Together they offer the reader a unified whole of language, form, and substance in which the poems mean more than the words they contain.

> From "April Thought" (p. 16)

> see how the daffodils
> lower their heads

like abandoned lovers
bereft of touch
when only yesterday
they thrived on tenderness

… remember how you thought
it would always be so

In traditional Japanese aesthetics, *wabi-sabi* is a view of the world based on acknowledgment of transience and imperfection. It has been described as beauty that is "perfectly imperfect." That sensibility is profoundly present as the poet reconciles with her losses, particularly her husband's death.

From "A New Season" (pp. 25-26)

alone
I am alone
that may always be so

this is not a poem about me

the lake is alive now
sun and wind play on the surface

I am alive
watch a new season arrive

sometimes this
is how
a love poem
ends

The poems in this collection embrace the *wabi-sabi* philosophy with a sense of insightful and hard-won acceptance by affirming that the imperfect, the impermanent, and the incomplete are important way stations on the journey toward wholeness.

Tiferet

From "Lesson from the Moon" (p. 28)

half a life still a dream
half a song lives on
half a meal can satisfy
half a moon shows how
                    half a light
is whole enough

Ebihara brings the collection to closure with a poem titled "Life Still." Significantly not "still life" as we generally understand the term, she plays on the word "still" and affirms what remains. In all of these poems, Ebihara gives witness to the process of reconstructing her life, creating "wonder from want" (p. 12), and accepting "the loneliness of singularity" (p. 23).

From "Life Still" (p. 29)

see how the Finch has no fear
of the Phoebe's call

she has her own voice

you're gone for months now
and I am a little less lost each day

if I believed in heaven
I would wish you here

on this hillside
with this music
in this peaceful
                    still
                    life

In this powerful collection, Ebihara offers her readers foundational encouragement for their own challenging journeys—an approach to gratitude for what has been and what is.

POETRY

Every River Remembers the Drowned

Lynn Domina

Remember that day
when you were not
afraid, when you watched
the sun
set across the river.
Remember how you knew night
would cool, though then
warm air still settled
across your shoulders
like your lover's arm
that time
when you were not afraid.
What are you afraid of today?
Not your lover or the sun's nature
burning your skin
or the river's nature
rising and rising and tumbling
across rocks and leaving
drowned dogs and raccoons and infants
in its wake.
What are you afraid of today?
Not the world's end, an apocalypse,
but this world, the one you live in
today, those people living behind your house
who have taken your house, your son,
who have set fire
to your house, and those people living
across the river
who lock their long arms together
and say nothing and say
don't step into the river, the river
is our river.

A Review of
Minglements: Prose on Poetry and Life
by Renée Ashley

BY ADELE KENNY

MINGLEMENTS: PROSE ON POETRY AND LIFE
by Renée Ashley
Del Sol Press, 2019
253 Pages
$14.44 Paperback
ISBN: 978-0-9998425-3-9
To order: https://smile.amazon.com/Minglements-
Prose-Poetry-Renee-Ashley/dp/0999842536/ref=sr_
1_1?keywords=minglements&qid=1565115864&s
=gateway&sr=8-1

Minglements—memories, relationships, entanglements—these (and more) are the subjects that Renée Ashley takes on in her most recent book. From the intriguing title to every page of this vast reservoir of wisdom and experience, Ashley spans the gap between memoir and literary analysis. She tackles the dominant tropes of a life in this hybrid work and takes her readers along for the ride. In the essays, analyses, reflections, reviews, and interviews, Ashley intermingles her personal and literary lives while challenging and inspiring readers to look beyond the merely factual to see what's real.

While Ashley's evocative "prose on poetry and life" unquestionably deepens appreciation for Ashley's work and for her world, it also causes the reader to look deeply into his or her own self. It dares the reader to think about the liminal spaces that lie, in all of our lives, between strength and weakness, depth and surface, past and present. Ashley makes it possible to see inside someone else's mind, to explore the many-shaded grays of who we are, and to achieve not only empathy but also connection.

"Our connections and associations help make the world easier both to comprehend and articulate. We compare, consciously or not; we draw or observe parallels. *This is like that,* we say. *This makes me think of that other thing*—similar to the kind of mapping that makes metaphor

work; perhaps, sometimes exactly the same kind. We recreate from our
context—not simply the current ambient circumstance or the location
in which our bodies, at any given moment, might take up space, but
the catalog of contexts we have absorbed throughout our lives—via those
accumulations, those personal and universal recognitions, sense-
and-memory associations with their fractional sameness—and whether
those connections rise up into our consciousness at any given time—say,
while you're writing a review of an essay on craft—that, no doubt is
another set of active connections, a subset of the whole and,
experientially, not the least bit irrelevant." (p. xiii)

Ashley discusses peripheral vision in one of the essays, but there's nothing tangential in her vision for this book. For example, when Ashley discusses her struggles with depression in the essay " Basic Heart: Depression and the Ordinary," the reader may think, "Oh, yeah, I know about depression." Ashley writes, "Writing is an act of finding out what I know, and this is what I know now: Depression *for me* is what is ordinary. I face some aspect of it every day." (p. 40) And the reader thinks, "I get that." Throughout, there is an underlying sense of feelings that are often disturbingly familiar.

When Ashley writes, "I have honed forgetting and silence into near perfections. They make my life more manageable" (p. 43), the reader asks, "Might that work for me?" The specific elements of our own lives may be vastly different, but there are many relatable things in this collection. Here is Ashley at her analytical, intellectual, and affective best. She tells the world who she is, that it's okay to be tough and vulnerable at the same time, and she tells us that we're not alone.

The idea that life is a shared experience, that we're all taking different paths up the same mountain, resonates strongly in the memoir portions of this book. The idea is that ultimately, on one level or another, observer and observed are one.

"Parts of you, you might feel, seem to be disappearing and you need to
further explore who you think you might be before you really do vanish
Middle-age, late middle-age, or an exceptional youth or youthful
narcissism is driving your bus. Listen, you're me one way or another.
You've got a ticket, what the hell. Why not?" (p. 53)

Tiferet

There are no "chapters" in this book, simply clearly delineated sections, analogous but each a special entity on its own. Reading cover to cover isn't prerequisite. Rather, skipping around, reading and reading again (the way one might read the *Bible* or a collection of poems) invites readers to choose whatever piques their interest.

In "A Possibility of Memoir," Ashley writes, "This is your life, you'll be saying to your reader. This is one draft of your life." (p. 60) And so it is with *Minglements*—an unflinching collection of thoughts on being that ratchets up life's tensions through nuanced scrutiny. Most noteworthy about Ashley's writing style is her ability to be both academic and unpretentious at the same time.

Underlying much of the book is Ashley's relationship with her mother and, often, the relationship strikes a kettledrum of knowing for the reader who finds something of his or her own "Ma" in Ashley's reflections (if not a mother then someone close who has defined the reader's personal grappling with loss and change). There is much in this book about the painful ferrying from one stage of life to another, and whatever good comes of it.

> "But Ma, alas, is no longer the very same Ma. …I am surprised and saddened that, while the rest of the world and me with it, is opening up by cyber-proxy and experience, Ma's world is shutting down, getting smaller all the time. And I see now just how much and how often I have been adjusting my gaze so that I might understand more of the world. I have been engaged, and that engagement, in a life that includes books about poems and in poems themselves, is also a good thing." (p. 127)

Later in the book, Ashley talks about her mother's death and the conditions of forgiveness.

> "It seems to me that I've never understood what forgiveness might actually entail, the parameters of the feeling or the act. Is it possible that her death had operated with a sort of automatic activation switch? Like the glass doors at the supermarket that you slide open when you weight-trip the switch to break the beam of light as you cross them? Might the vision of the softened aluminum bar have been a manifestation of forgiveness operating with the same sort of trigger? Because that's what it felt like.
> I'd always understood, I think, that she did the best she could." (p. 242)

Ashley's life is in the writing; the writing *is* Renée, the work is her process of surviving adversity and experience; and it's through her writing that Ashley drags understanding home by the scruff of its neck.

Throughout this collection, Ashley probes the compositional workings and talismanic calling of the creative process. At the same time, she also examines what it's like to teeter among resentment, remorse, and resilience. Just as she does in her poems, Ashley deftly pushes the literary and emotional envelopes with her prose. There's an electricity in her work that both shocks and warms her readers. In my review of another Ashley book, I compared her to Janis Joplin. In *Minglements*, Renée Ashley is Janis Joplin singing Puccini, and I don't want her to stop.

The Wall

Paul Genega

There's the remnant of a wall in the woods
I like to walk when the curtain of sleep rises early

Stones long ago toppled from places they fit tightly
Lay scattered in dimness daubed with lichen and moss

Some lean over like inebriated choristers
Others lay flat, staring back at the unblinking moon

There's no hint of what was walled in or walled out

No scar patch of pasture where vine and nettle thrive
No telling shards of cow horn or sheep jaw

The wall stands roughly three feet high
Though its height seems less important
Than the breath of its arc —

Glacial rubble stretching out on umber
Silvered at sunrise by spider webs and dew

The land seems all of one piece at the moment
But once, this wall insists, it was parceled
And divided, strictly cordoned by purpose and deed

On one side was something called mine
On the other yours or everyone's or no one's —

Hills, prairies, meadows, ravines…

Whitewater surging freely to the sea

There and then and here and now

Before there was a then and now
Before the gods bed down in leaf mold
Before the wall builders set sail

Tiferet Tifs

We are delighted to share our latest installment of Tiferet "Tifs". While a "tiff" is defined as a "petty argument", a "Tif" is anything but petty—it is a short exploration of a deeply meaningful subject. Our most recent theme for "Tiferet Tifs" was on "Faith." We asked authors to define their relationship to or understanding of faith and its role or absence in their lives. Here are a few of the responses we received. For more Tifs, please visit www.tiferetjournal. com.

Metaphysics of Faith
Phyllis Barber

Biblical scripture describes faith as the substance of things not seen—one of the best definitions. Faith means believing in something that hasn't happened yet, walking toward a light when you can't see what's behind it, expecting in something that might be beyond hope or speech.

Faith means believing, in a general way, something will happen. Specifics are troublesome, but if I have faith, I do my work with exceptional dedication, get out of my own way, and let things happen as they will. Faith is not dictation. It implies trust in the outcome—that it will be something useful, even wise, in the long run. That there will be twists and turns bigger than the self.

Faith is a belief in something shaped in dreams, something out of the ordinary, and unexpected. Faith is something yet to be.

Tiferet Tifs

Enlightenment
Carole Johannsen

When I was young, God was knowable. My church gave me adjectives to describe him—almighty, merciful and loving—and the Bible gave me the evidence in numbers: seven days of Creation, Ten Commandments, twelve apostles and 5,000 fed. God was good.

Later when I abandoned dogma, God lost gender and maybe some adjectives. I missed the God with structure. He who was predictable, knowable.

But now, when I unexpectedly see an impossibly vivid sunset, or when I pray with someone who's forgotten how to pray, and even when I rage at injustice and shake my fist at heaven—in those moments I believe in a way I did not, could not when I was young, that I am seen and heard by One who is always present.

I "know" so much less about God than I did in my once-upon-a-time youth, but I feel God's presence more deeply. If that is faith, then I am faithful. If it is not, then I am merely, profoundly thankful.

Tiferet Tifs

Faith
Siham Karami

To understand what faith is, one must understand the significance of the heart as the dwelling place of the soul or essence of a person. In Islam, the heart is where understanding occurs, possible if one thinks of consciousness as not being confined to the brain, but occupying the whole body and at its nucleus, the heart. There the soul/ consciousness processes thoughts, sensory input, memories, and emotions to form its core beliefs. So in that sense, all human beings have faith in something, and rely on that faith in both forming opinions and decision-making. Indeed the Quran refers to humans as "worshippers," from the divine perspective, regardless of their beliefs. Having faith, even to atheists who place their faith in empirical things, is hardwired into us. The name "Allah" *sounds* like the heartbeat; in the Quran this name is often and prominently followed by two names meaning Almighty, All-Merciful, like Yang the Creative and Yin the Receptive. From this, imagine Allah as the heartbeat of the universe, literally pulsing yang/yin of unimaginable energy. Faith in God puts us in tune with that pulse, spawning reverence and compassion in our *hearts*, filling our lives with meaning and fulfillment.

My Faith
Jane O'Shields-Hayner

My faith lies in orbitals and electrons. The child of an atheist, the niece of a scientist, I am skeptical to the bone.

As a child, I played with Petri dishes and beakers, culturing bacteria, dropping lifeless insects into formaldehyde and hearing disdain for anything that smelled of superstition. Included were the stories told in Baptist Sunday School, where my non-believing mother took me faithfully every Sunday.

Inversely, my life tells another story, for miracles open before me and I am startled, repeatedly, into a state of awe.

I have faith in the laws of the universe, yet statistical probability proves itself malleable in my life. In science and silence, I seek discernment, for in my experience, clarity, like the nucleus of an atom, lies in the center of every storm.

Faithful to a fault or unfaithful to an end, at times the fabric of my life winds about faith like knotted thread beneath a needle, but when the fray is sorted, I find nothing there.

Although my faith is nameless my life stretches toward it like iron shavings to a magnet and in simple symmetry, I rest in the field of faith.

Tiferet Tifs

Nothing to See Here
Julia Park Tracey

Nothing to see here. Not what you'd call "god." Just me and chickens and coffee and heat waves rising off the middle of the road while the doe pants in the woods, a psalm come to life; water drips off the vines I just watered and the speckled hen stands beneath looking up. Just go about your business. This is my summer noon. Bare feet, damp neck, jay screeching like a hawk, stealing peanuts off the rail.

The sun creeps over the canyon, nailing spiders and slugs and grasshoppers to the dirt. I have nothing to say because my words run out as through a funnel onto the page, papering a trail for this story that begs to be wrought. I peg my hair up with a pencil and scratch my back with a ruler. The red hen chuckles and purrs under the house. Dirt baths for everyone, and a stretch on the gravel in heat. The canopy of my cathedral sways most gently, two hundred feet above it all. When the wind blows, needles and feathers and leaves rain potpourri like grace upon my altar. The speckled hen pecks at water drops, at sowbugs, and scratches for seeds of something I can't name.

Faith
Jane Rosenberg LaForge

When I think of faith, I think of our father, delivering my sister and me to the synagogue each Saturday, to learn the Torah. We did not go to the reform temple as the other neighborhood kids did, but instead to the conservative one, where there was no reading or writing, or even the taking of attendance, on the Sabbath. Ours was all talk, memorization; I suppose much as it was in the world our father once inhabited, and his forefathers, where the study of Judaism could be forbidden or dangerous. Our father then drove home, to his bedroom and black and white television, to indulge in his first love: the movies of his childhood. Our father was deaf, due to an accident with explosives during adolescence. He often complained about contemporary culture, actors, music, and our high, childish voices: they rose far beyond his comprehension. Yet he was never disappointed by the film noirs he watched, the musicals, love stories and comedies. They were a balm, delivering dialogue he knew, songs he remembered. After we were grown, after the divorce, my sister's death and a spate of illnesses, those films were what best sustained him.

POETRY

From the Semi-Annual Cross-Stitch Conference, *Savvy Stitch*

Rogan Kelly

The bird died on a Thursday. She held it all night like an egg. Next morning, she packs the car with the bird in a cooler, wedges it in the middle console and drives to a conference in Jersey. Others went to dinner. She returns to the room where the winged body rests by the window: a grey vase of tulips on the sill beside. She pulls strips of lettuce from a turkey sandwich, collects part of the crust from the bread. And when she speaks to the empty room, her voice is the faint rusted creak of a half-hinged storm door before the wind picks up.

POETRY

How Did I Love Him

Susan Rich

at first sighting,   without   language or need—

at second sight—
as if he had already torn a piece,

exhumed the pink inside of me—

In a millet field—

without knowledge—

I conjured him from dust and air:

orphaned gecko, violet flame—

from our first nakedness in the desert,

to our nonstop ribbon of talk

like a three-dimensional arc

of tragedy, a lightning rod, a quasar of hunger?

Why did I love him /

across the equator / on a freight train / in a failing jeep—

once upon a time in a Mopti whorehouse

Tiferet

as the bartender prayed

while conducting low-paid women up the watchful limbs

of the baobab tree.

Who was it that loved him /

to abstraction— like a private detective, an African reggae band—

Next time / there will be no next time/

I would barricade the continent—

double-lock the windows and floors

to all that breathed in me—

plug my ears to his baritone psalms, his siren pleas.

POETRY

Crossing the Andes into New Jersey

Tom Plante

Somehow or other, a postage stamp
valued at three centavos finds its way

from Argentina to my basement in a
sack of wild bird seed. I fish the pale

green stamp from the seed in the
final scoop and wonder who the man

in the portrait is. Of course, I have to
look him up to find out that he was

Jose de San Martin—liberator of
Argentina, Chile, and Peru, who

crossed the Andes with an army, with
Bernardo O'Higgins and, later, with

Simon Bolivar, to free the people of
South America from Spanish rule.

Meanwhile … the cardinals and
chickadees wait for me.

POETRY

This Time

James Crews

This time, I'd take my mother's hand
as she stepped into the viewing room,
my father lying with fingers intertwined
in the casket no one told me would be open.
This time, I'd keep her from stumbling
on the burgundy carpet, and I'd be
what she reached for to steady herself,
instead of an empty chair. And when she
nearly fell upon seeing him there like that,
giving a yelp as if her leg had been caught
in a trap, I'd know my parents were
more in love than I ever imagined.
If I could go back now, I'd arc an arm
against the small of her back, and become
the husband for a moment, our grief
a single thing slung across our shoulders,
two buckets swinging on either side,
almost too heavy to bear as we approach
the open casket, each of us now
holding one of his hands.

NONFICTION

Finding Temporary Refuge in Islam

Ilona Fried

The old city of Marrakesh, the Medina, seethes rather than soothes. Nature is largely absent except for countless cats, darting birds, crowing roosters and braying donkeys. Men and women atop sputtering mopeds and rickety bicycles maneuver in tight spaces, a hair's breadth from pedestrians. Horses and pack mules appear around tight corners, hauling large loads. Porters and vendors push wide carts through the maze. Like water in a river, the flow of people adjusts; the chaos rarely becomes congestion. The lack of ego refreshes, even though I choked on the fumes.

Shortly after arriving to a traditional Marrakesh *riad* for a month-long international co-working retreat, a soft voice dropped in: "Love this place." It felt like a spiritual assignment, where "love" did not mean swooning over the nerve-jangling madness I typically avoid, but offering my attention without judgment.

The Medina might as well be from another era, if not a different universe, compared to the modern French quarter of Marrakesh. The latter is home to sophisticated cocktail bars, upscale eateries, modern supermarkets, department stores and asphalt roads teeming with taxis, buses and cars. In the often unpaved streets and alleys of the old city, thick smoke wafts from street stalls where men grill and roast meats, including sheep heads and stuffed spleen. Wizened shopkeepers perch on stools behind tiny storefronts and take cash only, yet trust you'll pay the next day if you're a few *dirhams* short. Young men with nothing to do and nowhere to go act as unwanted tour guides, trailing visitors and telling them what to do and where to go before asking for a handout. Many men and women wear *djellabas*, shapeless long tunics with peaked hoods, called *qob*. At first the garments looked like pajamas, but after noticing how versatile they were for Morocco's weather, a mercurial mix of cold, wind, rain and sun, I wanted one, too.

On a drizzly day I dodged puddles and runoff as I went searching for this hooded garment. After trying on bulky full-length versions in somber browns and grays, and carefully and politely extricating myself from the eager vendor's stall, I visited another shop whose employee, an energetic man in a peacock blue *djellaba*, waved me inside. I hoped he had others in that color. He didn't, but after much deliberation and negotiation I purchased a shorter, cape-like version in slate blue, and a bright red wool scarf for extra warmth. The seller gently wrapped the scarf around my head in traditional Berber style, giving me a mysterious air. I snapped a selfie so I could recreate the look later. In Morocco, to dress like a local is considered a sign of appreciation, not appropriation, and simply knowing that filled me with enormous relief.

My fellow global nomads said my cape suited me and my complexion. Wearing it suited my soul. The act of slipping it over my head brought me more closely into a state of immersion, allowing me to drop beneath my Western persona, my predilections and even my anxieties. My critical "I" took a back seat to the eyes of a more neutral and compassionate observer. Choosing to appear a bit more like the people around me dissolved some of my sense of otherness. My basic French allowed me to interact with shopkeepers and vendors. To explore on my own felt more compelling than hanging out with the group, who seemed more drawn to modern Marrakesh and to the tourist-oriented eateries of the old city.

Early in the trip, needing time alone to recover from jet lag, I peeled away from the others and had lunch at a basic booth around the corner from our *riad*. This stall sold fried sardines and *tagines*, foods cooked in a clay pot. The fresh-faced proprietor, with a short beard and a skullcap, prepared the dishes in a small oven and grill near the street. I didn't see a posted menu so I asked him the price of the sardines: 4 *dirham* (40 cents) apiece. After he gave me a sample, I ordered several and a glass of mint tea. I sat down at one of a handful of small plastic tables behind him. He asked if I wanted salad. I nodded. He brought over what looked like salsa alongside chopped red onions. Unaware that locals used bread as utensils, I asked him for a knife, fork and napkin. It took him several minutes to track them down and, once he did, I quickly devoured the food. Whenever I passed his often empty stall after that, we greeted each other. Unlike many Moroccan Muslims, he even allowed me to take a photo of him and his wife.

That I chose the grit of the Medina over more glamorous and trendy venues made me think of the *midrash* (ancient commentary) on the story of baby Moses. It is said that while playing on the Egyptian ruler's lap, Moses reached for the Pharaoh's shiny, jewel-encrusted crown. Afraid of losing his throne, the paranoid Pharaoh asked his counselors the meaning of the infant's action. Some said the baby should be killed immediately. One advisor suggested testing the child by placing two bowls nearby, one filled with glowing coals, another with gold and jewels, to see which he would choose. An angel directed the infant to reach for the coal. Moses put the burning ember in his mouth, forever impairing his speech but sparing his life. While I am no prophet or soothsayer, I am an introvert who can get tongue-tied in fast moving group conversations; I'm often more comfortable in silence or in one-on-one interactions. To wander on my own, apart from the others, felt like a self-muting within the group and, also, a way to spare my true self from feigning interest in activities and places I didn't enjoy.

My sense of orientation adjusted faster than I expected. The once maddeningly maze-like lanes of the Medina eventually imprinted themselves in my nervous system as an inner map. Wandering them, day after day, had a similar effect as walking a labyrinth, whose sacred geometry can invite meditative states. Once my body knew where to go, my vigilance softened enough so I could focus more of my attention on what I wanted to see. It wasn't until I visited the Majorelle Gardens, once owned by Yves Saint-Laurent and now a major tourist site in modern Marrakesh, and found myself startled by throngs of pose-striking and selfie-taking tourists, that I realized how quickly I had become accustomed to, if not enamored of, the Medina. Its old world ways and mesmerizing parade of life that streamed through its narrow streets offered a compelling antidote to the newsfeed that, at home, could hijack my attention.

In early evening, overstimulated by the smells and sounds of the old city, I often returned to the *riad* just as others were preparing for a night on the town. Tucked behind a darkened doorway at the end of a narrow alley, our *riad*, like other traditional buildings, had a flat roof overlooking the city. On clear days, it offered views of the snow-capped Atlas Mountains. In what became a ritual, I climbed to the top as muezzins at nearby mosques chanted the *adhan*, the call to prayer. Transmitted over crackling loudspeakers affixed to the top of towers, the five daily invocations acted as a raucous reminder, above the bustle of the city, for people on the ground to stop, at least for a while, and consider that "God is greatest." I made a point in those moments to pause and pay closer attention to my surroundings. I inhaled scents of cooking that wafted up from the streets and from neighboring buildings. I tracked the movements of cats who silently slipped between rooftops like stealthy spies. I watched swirls of clouds turn pink, orange and then a deep purple against a fading blue sky. The prayers and faith of others, transmitted via heartfelt gutturals through the air, helped me savor and bear witness to the completion of a day. Some nights, after the sky darkened, I walked a few hundred feet to a bustling stretch of the neighborhood and, after peeking inside a vendor's pot or spotting something tasty on a grill, chose to have a small bite at a stall. Often I was the only woman and the only foreigner yet, without exception, I was always made to feel welcome and valued. Even some of the more cramped eateries had shown greater hospitality than some of the tourist-oriented venues where Western-friendly menus and amenities were served with a chilly indifference.

The more I witnessed Islam up close, or more closely than I'd ever been able to, and the more local merchants I met who prayed each day, the less "other" it became. Although I had spent a month in Jerusalem in 2007, at the time I had been trying and failing to connect more deeply with Judaism and, out of both ingrained prejudice and a lack of time, hadn't paid Islam much attention. In Marrakesh, the calls to prayer, which frequently woke me in the mornings and accompanied me throughout the day and into the evening, became anchors of my experience. Occasionally I found myself outside of mosques during prayer and, through open doorways, lingered to both observe and absorb. In one house of worship in the middle of the *souk*, the market area of the Medina, men squeezed shoulder to shoulder as they prostrated themselves. In the few years I attended synagogue after my father passed away, we prostrated ourselves during the High Holy Days only, a rare ritual that felt awkward. Many congregants didn't want to or couldn't lower themselves to the ground, and the lack of full participation diminished the impact of what might have been an otherwise powerful gesture of surrender. Yet watching these men pray and, without any self-consciousness, place their foreheads on the floor, offered solace by osmosis. As a non-Muslim and a woman, I couldn't join them. To know that at least part of the world unhooked from the frenzy five times a day, took off their shoes and prayed, gave me hope that perhaps I, with a racing mind that often got ahead of itself, could learn to do something similar.

* * *

The sprawling *souk*, with each of its many tiny alleys filled with enough merchandise, colors, textures and scents to captivate a visitor for hours, could be endlessly explored. Therefore it's a small miracle that I eventually stumbled across a cluster of eateries tucked into a nondescript nook between a corridor of slipper vendors and a group of Moroccan lamp shops. I asked a mustachioed man wearing an apron to show me what was cooking in each of his three pots, arranged over a burner. He lifted each of the cone-shaped clay lids of the *tagines* in turn: Sardines. Chicken. Beef. I asked for the sardines, whose skin glinted like silver amidst tomatoes, carrots, olives and potatoes. With the sun out, the proprietor mentioned I could sit on the roof. I climbed two flights of narrow steps only to discover a group of smoking tourists so I returned to ground level for cleaner air. As I sat facing the entrance, I noticed a television attached high on the wall, near the ceiling, its screen blank save for two words: *Palestine Quraan*. As I settled in, I listened to the imam. Even though I did not understand any of it, in the quality of his voice I sensed his reverence and heartfelt beliefs. Rather than block it out, I let the rhythmic undulations wash over me as if they were from a Jewish *niggun*, a soothing wordless chant.

Delighted and nourished by the food, I returned a few days later when it was raining. The closed rooftop meant limited space. Another customer, a man in an impeccably hand-stitched *djellaba* and knit skullcap, offered to share his small table with me. As I ate my meal, a local specialty of beef slow-cooked with lemon in a clay pot, I remarked in French upon its deliciousness. My dining neighbor said the food was "beautiful," a word I would not have chosen yet, given the kindness of the man who prepared and served it, felt accurate. After I finished eating, I listened again to the live *Quraan* broadcast. While digesting, I asked the chef if he always tuned into that station. He said yes, it's better than television with its noise and violent shows. That he also prized calm and tranquility made me feel as if I had found, in a person whose life was very different from mine, a kindred spirit. I was sorry I hadn't located his oasis sooner.

Towards the end of my stay, as the weather became warmer, I purchased a thin red scarf as a *hijab* to cover my hair. I hoped it would protect me from the elements and buy me a bit of peace, shielding me from the exhausting onslaught of hawkers. Having already experimented with the Berber-style head wrap, I wanted to experience covering myself this way, too. Would it feel empowering, transforming or make me feel as if I were disappearing? After draping and tying the scarf the way I'd been shown by the man who sold it to me, I snapped a selfie. Despite the cheerful color, I looked solemn and deadened, not chic or elegant like many Muslim women I'd seen around town. Still, even though the *hijab* did not suit me or lift my spirits, I decided to wear it. The scarf temporarily fooled a group of German tourists I bantered with in the *souk* as they shopped for slippers.

As I strolled about the market, one food vendor tried to reel me in to eat at his stall. I told him, in French, I wasn't hungry and kept moving, but still he confronted me.

"Are you Moroccan?" he asked in French.

"No," I said.

"Where are you from?"

"The United States."

"No, before that." His voice was insistent. "Where are you from?"

"Europe," I said. My father had been born in Hungary and had been the only member of his family to survive Auschwitz.

"You have an Arab face," he said. "Are you one of us?"

He looked at me. I looked at him. A primordial fear of being the hated and hunted "other," a fear I had not sensed in quite some time, stirred in the core of my being. I remembered that my father, when I was a college student in the late 1980s, told me not to wear a Star of David when flying overseas in case the plane was hijacked. Contrary to Hebrew School indoctrination and Jewish martyrology, my father believed it was better to be inconspicuous and survive than to proclaim one's Jewishness and perish. When he was alive, I largely kept my ethnicity, and my limited practice of Judaism, to myself, mentioning it only to friends and close associates. It had been neither a secret nor a prominent pillar of my existence. As this man and I stared at each other, I wondered what my life might have been like had I either embraced my religion unequivocally or rejected it outright, rather than letting it live in the shadows most of the time.

"*Je suis Juif,*" I said.

That "I am Jewish" spilled from my mouth in French startled me. Had my head scarf, which I hoped would conceal my foreignness, forced me to reveal it instead? Was my ancestry truly written all over my face for those who are fascinated by eyes, noses, jaws and cheekbones? "Jewish" is not an identity I prioritize over other aspects of my being. Like the full length *djellaba* I didn't buy, Judaism feels like an awkward, ill-fitting garment. I don't keep kosher or engage in specifically Jewish practices. To tell someone I am Jewish feels incomplete. My sense of self is dynamic, not fixed by bloodline. Not everyone understands that. And, not everyone likes Jews. I wasn't sure how this man would react, but at that point I was too tired to care.

"Welcome," he said. "Welcome."

It's as if he had waved a magic wand, zapping my primordial fear.

* * *

A few days before I left Marrakesh I walked towards the stall where, nearly four weeks before, I sat on a plastic chair and ate fried sardines. As I approached I did a double take. Two pairs of foreigners ate at this once empty place. They sat on wood and woven straw stools with matching tables, furniture common to tourist-oriented eateries. Bamboo-like wall coverings added ambience to the tiny stall. A chalkboard with a posted menu rested outside; it listed couscous, *tagines*, and brochettes, but no sardines. The proprietor, wearing a baseball cap rather than a skullcap, waved at me. I crossed the narrow street and stepped into his booth. I asked him what happened to the sardines. He said they didn't smell good and, because he wanted to attract tourists, he decided to stop serving them. His redesigned restaurant had been open for just a day. I told him how surprised I was to see the new look, which I barely recognized. His was the first establishment on the roughly paved street to telegraph "tourist friendly," even though many other food stalls and vendors had been quite welcoming and even generous with me. I didn't begrudge him his decision yet I felt strangely sad about it, as if his small renovation were a harbinger of accelerated change. Since I had come to love the gritty, devout neighborhood, and even became accustomed to the smoke-belching mopeds, I couldn't bear to imagine that one day the area might become more sanitized and gentrified and, potentially, less chaotic, congenial and warm.

For a moment I believed that the particulars of this place had given it the qualities of home, a spot I would think of fondly and even miss. I had forgotten that, in choosing to experience this small corner of the planet through the eyes of love, I had allowed it be a temporary refuge. Perhaps if I could remember to "love this place" wherever I happened to be, the whole world could become a sanctuary.

FICTION

Unaccompanied Minor

Angela Bean

Though I've interviewed thousands of aliens in detention, I've never interviewed detained kids, especially when they look exactly like mine at that age. Except for the eyes. The *ojos* peering out of this child have the dimmer on low, as if he were in a dark room. Not here, not in this hot chamber of howling children. The boy sits in one of the cheapo plastic Walmart chairs strewn around the room, feet together like praying hands swinging three inches above ground. He's next to an empty card table. On it is a lone straw-stabbed juice box.

I'm wearing my summer regulation ICE short sleeves that have my name Martinez stitched on the pocket. It's plastered to my back and I can feel sweat coalescing at the nape of my neck. The room smells like tears and snot and little kid pee. Other than that, it looks like a day care center, bean bag pillows, soft dolls and plush animals strewn around the floor. But there is no mistaking this place; it's a jail complete with gun loaded guards at the door.

"Hey, I'm Juan," I say in Spanish. The file says he's from Honduras. Pudgy, his dark matted hair drapes over his forehead. His fat cheeks shelve eyes like onyx stones. I look around. Where is his assigned social worker from the Office of Refugee Resettlement? How long has he been waiting here? I feel late, like the parent who misses the six o'clock pick up.

I drag over another chair from an empty card table and sit across from the boy.

"Are you Alberto?" I say. He looks startled. " Hey, don't be scared, I'm just going to talk to you about your trip here."

Trip, shit, as if he'd hopped a plane to LA. I know how to talk to those kids, the ones I inspect at the airport. You ask them if they're going to Disneyland. Not little Alberto though. He was rounded up in the desert near the border with his mother. They had a plastic bag full of sleeves of crackers, a fleece blanket and a half gallon of water between them. God knows where the mother is by now. Alberto's in custody at Tornillo, a tent city outside of El Paso. Stashed children. I check his birthday, July 15, 2010. He's nine years old. What the fuck. I hate this detail. Refugee camps in America.

"Tito, my name is Tito," says the boy.

I look down at the open file and see a picture of Alberto/Tito. It's clearly this kid. I check again for the adult who is supposed to be looking out for him from ORR. His supposed guardian angel. I feel icy all of a sudden, as if the guardians in this room are all Lucifer's agents. Tito looks at me, his eyes suddenly brighten, and I see flecks of brown in them like the sun is coming out from inside his head.

"Alberto is *mi papá.*"

"Are you the oldest brother in your family, Tito?" I swallow hard. Martinez, for God's sake, man-up, don't lose your shit.

"*Si*"

"Okay, I understand. You came here with your *mamá* right? Who were you coming to see?"

He says nothing. His eyes return to before, the brown flecks are gone, and his lower lip quivers. I know that lip and I want to take him onto my lap and tell him it's going to be okay. But I don't. We've been told not to touch them, and the training script runs through my head. *Don't be fooled. These children are pawns of their parents, nothing more than baby illegals who will grow up to become big criminals.* I see him missing his mother, but the little man isn't going to cry. The lip stops wobbling. Tightens. He's been through a lot. Anyone can see that. I feel like God and the Devil are duking it out in me. But my job is to find out if he has any people here, other than the mother who is in Federal lockup. If this had happened to my grandma, my ass would be parked in Michoacán hiding from my cousins in the cartel. Or I'd be deep in it.

"Hey, Tito do you want more juice?" He doesn't answer. His brows come together, collecting his rebellion. The silent treatment. I can't threaten him with anything worse than he's already experienced in the last two weeks. I continue to read the file while Tito rests his head on his crossed arms.

FICTION

Beyond the Ghetto Gates

(an excerpt)

Michelle Cameron

March 1796
Ancona, Italy

Tall buildings loomed on either side of the ghetto street. Mirelle was used to the narrow space, but today the air seemed more fetid than usual, the close-packed homes more menacing. The buildings—many built centuries before and precariously expanded upward—were crumbling at their foundations. Apartments exuded the smells of a hundred cooking pots, paint curling under the sweat and filth of packed living.

Toddlers played in the streets, ignoring the refuse running down the center sewer. Housewives stopped to gossip, straw baskets crushed against their sides. The market was bustling, with vibrant oranges and lemons piled into pyramids, cut citrus samples sharp in the spring air, bundled chard and spinach, flowery clusters of cauliflower and broccoli, and long spears of artichokes piled high. Crusty breads, fruit-filled flans, and boxes of biscotti wafted enticing odors. But today all Mirelle felt were the centuries of dirt and sweat trapped inside the enclosed ghetto. The walls pressed in on her, making it difficult to breathe. On impulse, she decided to visit a different market—the one outside the gates, where she could feel sea breeze and sunlight on her face.

During daylight hours, the ornate, wrought-iron gates at the ghetto entrance were flung wide. Because her friend Dolce often designated them as a meeting spot, Mirelle knew their every nook and curve. As she'd wait, she'd run her fingers over the peeling patterns, twisting and curling. From dawn until nightfall, ghetto residents moved freely through the stone archway into the city of Ancona. As the sun dipped behind the horizon, however, city guards slammed the gates shut and chained a heavy padlock to the bars. The clang of the closing gates always raised the hair on the back of Mirelle's neck.

It affected her carefree brother even more. Jacopo often railed against being imprisoned inside the ghetto. "I want to see what the sea looks like under the stars," he'd admitted one night as they stood outside, straining to see the few inches of night sky visible to them. "I want to walk freely out the gate and not have someone stare at me because I'm Jewish."

Something had stirred in her chest as he spoke. A whole world existed outside the ghetto. If only they could both walk out of the gates freely.

But they were trapped. Day or night, whenever the Jews left their homes, they were required by law to don the yellow hat and armband that branded them as different. For as long as she could remember, Mirelle had covered her brown locks with a yellow kerchief before walking the streets. She would wrinkle her nose in the mirror as she adjusted the badge of her faith. *They make us wear yellow because it is the color of urine*, she'd think distastefully. *And of cowardice.*

Her brother might feel caught inside the enclosure of the locked ghetto gates, but she felt doubly trapped—as a Jewish woman.

Catching sight of the open gateway, she tossed her head high and walked through. The street led straight to the quay, where the Gentiles gathered to sell their produce. She would have to buy kosher meat and bread on her way home, but she could buy fresh fruit and vegetables and eggs here.

As she neared the water, she took a deep breath. Early spring air mixed with the salty tang of the sea. The piercing cry of gulls and the shouts of men working on the docks drifted up. The quay was alive with the bustle of sailors and housewives, beautiful, glass-fronted shops, and busy coffeehouses.

Mirelle made her way toward the market stalls. She'd just started to select some brown eggs from a smiling woman when a man rudely elbowed past her.

"Francesca Marotti!" he cried. "A word!"

"Good morning, Signor Russo." Signora Marotti's fingers, gripping the wooden cross at her neck, belied her calm tone. "I'll attend you after I wait on this customer."

Signor Russo, a rough-looking man with a sour expression, glared at Mirelle, cold eyes lingering on her kerchief and armband. He sneered. "She can wait."

Mirelle felt a protest rising but closed her lips against the rush of words. Anything she said would just sharpen his hatred. She was nothing more than dirt beneath his feet, all because she was a Jewess and he a Catholic.

Even the market woman, noticing the man's scornful glance at Mirelle's Jewish insignia, lost her kind smile. "You'll have to wait," she said to Mirelle, without a trace of apology in her voice. "What is it, Signor Russo?"

"Where is your husband, Signora Marotti? I've been looking for him for three days."

Tiferet

The woman squared her shoulders. "Where should he be but at home, tending to our acres?"

"Do you think me an idiot?" the man spat. "I've been there already. He's not home."

"You're mistaken," Signora Marotti replied. "He promised me—"

"You're a fool." Signor Russo laughed humorlessly. "I trusted his promises, and where did they get me? He owes me, Signora. He owes half of Ancona, I hear, but I'm the one he'll pay."

"Talk to him." The woman's hand clutched her crucifix, knuckles turning white. "I can't help you. Why are you bothering me and my customers?"

"Your customers?" Signor Russo looked Mirelle over, disgust writ large on his face.

Once again, Mirelle bit back her words.

"I'll take whatever money you've earned this morning, Signora. And I'll be back later today to collect the rest. As part payment of what's due me."

Signora Marotti gasped in anger. "You'd rob an innocent woman—pregnant besides"—Mirelle's eyes went to the woman's slightly protruding midriff—"and her young daughter?"

"I'll have what I'm owed. Let it be a lesson to you."

He extended a hand, and Mirelle watched as the woman slowly reached into her apron to retrieve the few soldi she'd earned that morning.

"And you," Signor Russo said, pocketing the money and turning on Mirelle. "Give me the money you were going to pay for the eggs."

Mirelle thought fast. "I already paid her."

"That's right, she did," Signora Marotti agreed.

Their eyes met for a second, then both glanced away.

"Pah! This is all you've made this morning? Pitiful. I'll be back this evening—and you'd better be here. And tell your husband that he has until the end of the week to finish paying off his debt—or else." He stomped off.

The women watched his retreating back. When he'd turned a corner, Mirelle counted out the coins for the eggs. "I'll take some artichokes, too," she said, though she hadn't planned to.

Signora Marotti nodded, her face pale. She slipped the coins into the neck of her blouse. "Thank you," she whispered.

Maybe she doesn't have to wear yellow, but she's as trapped as I am, Mirelle thought as she made her way back to the ghetto. *Jew or Gentile, we women must do as we're told.*

POETRY

Path

Miriam Berkley

The path is obscure.
I could follow it blind.
The summer grass whispers
Against my knees.
I have learned, too,
The touch of this air
Upon my lips.

I am early.
You stand in the doorway.
The room.
The bed.
Tenderness
And joy.

The flush and fade of sky,
Slap of the night wind,
(Soon, leaf upon the ground)
I know this path,
This sad dimension
That leads away from you.

NONFICTION

The Oven

Teresa H. Janssen

The boys would be celebrating their tenth and twelfth birthdays that spring. I wanted to bake them cakes, but we didn't have an oven. When we had arrived in Ecuador a few months before to do a year of medical volunteer work, we had moved into a spare one-bedroom apartment containing a refrigerator and gas stove. It was adequate, but I wanted an oven.

My husband asked around the hospital and heard that someone was moving and wanted to sell his propane oven. I started dreaming about baked potatoes, pizzas, and pies.

"We can sell you our oven at the end of the month," the soft-spoken bookkeeper told him. "My wife and I are going to the States. We are going to look for work in California."

Thousands of Ecuadorians went to work in the States during the years we lived there—the majority undocumented. This migration was spurred by an economic collapse caused by a slide in oil revenues, combined with bank failures, and an inflation rate that devalued the Ecuadorian currency by sixty-five per cent. Many villages became 'widow towns' of women and girls, old men, and young boys. Though the economy had improved, no one trusted it. No wonder the bookkeeper believed working in the States was his only chance to get ahead.

The next week, he and his wife, a pediatric nurse, came to our apartment. They were a handsome couple in their mid-thirties. They asked us if we would consider writing letters of recommendation for them.

The nurse looked around our apartment. She scanned our new dishes, the stack of children's board games, and the shelf of books along the kitchen wall.

"We want our children to be able to go to university. Our work here doesn't pay enough for us to afford their tuitions. We are flying to Mexico City, and then we will travel to the border."

She told me their three children would be staying with their grandparents in the capital while they were gone. She gazed out the kitchen window at the children on the street below playing in front of their homes and turned away.

"You don't have visas?" I said.

"No, we will pay someone to take us across."

My stomach turned.

"Do you speak English?" I asked.

They shook their heads.

"What work will you do?" my husband said.

"Oh, anything. Cleaning. Washing. Yardwork. We will save money for three years and then come back."

Three years was an eternity. We had only been in Ecuador for three months, and I was already homesick. How could they manage such a long time away from their children? I felt a physical ache, as though I'd been jabbed in the stomach, at the thought of their long separation. I looked up into the woman's eyes. All my thoughts were reflected and more—determination. Didn't I have the same hopes and dreams of education and opportunity for my children?

I agreed to write the letters. I typed one for each of them and made several copies. I said we knew them from the hospital where they were respected employees.

I thought of the heat and the lack of water and of all that could happen during their journey to the border. Would they make it across?

I wrote that they were good, honest people needing to pay for their children's schooling.

Would they ever see their children again?

I wondered who would read my letters. A San Diego construction boss looking for unskilled labor who didn't speak enough English to complain? A busy mother in L.A. looking for a cheap cleaning lady? I signed my name with my address and phone number in the U.S. I wondered which of us would make it across the border first.

They invited us to dinner to thank us for the recommendations. Their children had already gone to their grandparents, so we left our kids at home. We walked down the hill to their small cinder-block house, sat at the kitchen table, and drank beer. We tried to give them tips about life in the States, about how to find a place to live, about looking for jobs and getting around. We didn't know where to begin.

They told us about the rainy season in Ecuador, about the showers to come that would green up the brown hills almost overnight and turn dust into mud.

We talked about snow.

The nurse went to the kitchen and brought out dinner: soup, boiled potatoes, long slices of yucca, and two roasted guinea pigs—an Ecuadorian delicacy reserved for special occasions. The rodents lay on white plates with little eyes closed, teeth sticking out and tiny paws clutching the air. They been had roasted in the hot oven, until their skins browned into crisp outer coatings. I struggled to chew the desiccated meat. I couldn't avoid the sadness in the eyes of our hosts who had stopped talking and were merely picking at this final meal.

I knew they had weighed the risks before committing to the journey. I was moved that there were not enough compelling reasons for them to stay. I knew they would begin new lives—in shadows.

My forebears had left Ireland for similar reasons—oppression by their government, hopes for a better life, dreams for their children. They had been given wakes by their families before they departed, for fear they would never return, (and none did.) Arriving nearly penniless, they had become outsiders in a new land, working as maids, laundresses, road builders and deliverymen. But in those times, they had been allowed to bring their children and had been welcomed by a country that had valued their labor and been willing to give them a chance.

No one was able to lift the somber mood at the table, not even my husband who was usually able to coax a smile from our most miserable child. The pain came back, like a toothache in my gut, and I lost my appetite. I forced down the meal with another glass of beer, then our hosts lugged in the metal box that was their oven, we paid them, called a taxi, loaded it, wished them good-bye and good luck, and rode home in silence.

I felt like a vulture—scavenging the remains of the latest family tragedy. I rushed through the doorway of our apartment, while my husband tottered behind me carrying the heavy appliance. I searched for our children and hugged them—bowled over by my privilege.

The oven sat on my kitchen counter. I baked birthday cakes and cookies, but the oven ran hot, and despite my vigilance, my confections often burned and tasted of grit. I was relieved to leave the oven behind when we flew home with our children at the end of the year.

We never heard from the Ecuadorian couple. I never learned whether they made it to the border, found work, or reunited with their children. I think about them when I bake a birthday cake, attend a graduation, or hear news of children separated from their parents—the penalty we exact these days from those without means who journey to the border to escape oppression or pursue a dream. It brings back the ache that just won't leave.

NONFICTION

Sentences

Karl Plank

After Layli Long Soldier

This is a sentence: a sequence of words or a statement that is complete.

This, too, is a sentence: the pronouncement of a punishment that states the conditions under which one will live and be regarded for a period of time.

The first describes a unit of grammar; the second, an instance of its practice, as when an authority utters a sentence that judges another as guilty, lacking something necessary, or different from what is desired.

We associate the first with teachers, writers, and linguists, but the second with judges and officials of government who have power to use *sentence* as a verb.

When authorities use *sentence* as a verb, they employ it to say *you are,* for example, *a prisoner, an alien, someone unwelcome in our company, one of the shameful, one of the dead.*

You will live there and not here or *You will live in this way* fairly paraphrase what authorities mean when they use *sentence* as a verb.

Though these have subjects and verbs, such sentences are incomplete in ways that matter, saying at once too much and not enough.

A sentence may be technically complete, but not just or true or whole.

Juan Francisco Trevino, the governor of New Mexico in 1675, sentenced 47 Pueblo medicine men to be flogged, humiliated, imprisoned and sold into slavery for practicing sorcery; he sentenced some of these to death, hanging them in Jemez, Nambé Pueblo, and San Felipe.

Tiferet

The governor used *sentence* as a verb to make *sorcery* a form of *idolatry* and to make those who practiced it dead men.

The Pueblo medicine men had their own sentences to speak, such as *When Jesus came, the Corn Mothers went away.*

One of the punished, the Tewa Popé, led the Pueblo revolt of 1680 so that the Corn Mothers might return.

The preceding sentence also means that he drove out the Spanish, the friars, and their ways to please the Corn Mothers.

This lasted for a period of twelve years until *La Reconquista*.

With *La Reconquista*, Don Diego de Vargas, the new Spanish governor, renamed the mission's wooden madonna *La Conquistadora*, or *she who conquers*.

A panel of the bronze doors of the basilica in Santa Fe shows the rescue of the wooden madonna, a building on fire, and the date 1680, but does not refer to the Corn Mothers.

A tour guide at the Taos Pueblo says "some say we have been here for a thousand years, but we believe we have been here since *time immemorial.*"

What *some say* and what she says are different kinds of sentences.

She means that the story of their being here goes back to the beginning, beyond remembered time.

This story speaks of the Mothers planting seeds in the underground and seeds growing and breaking through to light.

The Mothers followed the growth to emerge from *Shipapu,* the center of the world beneath the earth's surface.

Before the revolt, Popé sent out runners to the pueblos, each runner bearing knotted ropes.

The Pueblo were to untie one knot each day until there were no knots left.

At that point, they would know it was time to begin the revolt.

Some sentences are spoken this way, without words.

A knotted rope is also a ladder.

In the pueblo, ladders lead down into the *kiva,* the chamber beneath the ground where one speaks as the subject of sentences not heard by others above.

The *kiva* is *Shipapu,* the place beneath, from which the Mothers emerged.

Ladders lead to *time immemorial.*

Like the Corn Mothers themselves, the other story surfaces from the *kiva* that is underground.

The other story makes ordinary sentences incomplete.

Those who use *sentence* as a verb cannot coexist with the *kiva.*

Their sentences are superficial.

It should not surprise that *kivas* were desecrated and destroyed during the *Conquista,* sentenced to perish.

It should not surprise that they did not perish.

The dead also go under the ground.

It is where we go, the living and the dead, to complete our sentences.

We go to the world that is *under* to find beginnings and ends, to hear the words the Mothers, the very old, and the fallen say for themselves.

These are not historical statements about Pueblos and *Conquistadores,* as much as warnings to ourselves:

Tiferet

That there is always another word spoken elsewhere;

(That our sentences need this word)

That the earth cracks open, in portals to hidden sanctuaries, to reveal what is deep and beneath and beyond,

What is emerging.

NONFICTION

Infusion

Diana Tokaji

> *Pliny, the Elder, a Roman naturalist (AD 23-79),*
> *believed Borage, or Starflower, to be an anti-depressant,*
> *and it has long been thought to give*
> *courage and comfort*
> *to the heart.*

1.

I've come to Germany for a week of treatments because I've been inexplicably trembling for years. The clinic and these intravenous infusions are my hope, but suddenly I cannot imagine offering my arm. Not even to the German nurse with her V-neck whites and kind smile, or the Hungarian one with frosted hair and the energy of eight of me.

I can no longer imagine the tender fold, the choice of veins, the butterfly needle, the intravenous flood; even the easy chair, so comforting with a foot stool and slight recline, the fan on at just the right distance. I have eaten their food with such gusto, delighted by the freshness, and this confuses me. Their food tastes of gentle cooking. Of love, actually.

2.

> *ACHTUNG! ATTENTION!*
> *Do not exit without your key, as this door to the garden locks behind you.*

I do not know German. Yet the word, *ACHTUNG!* slaps me, as if the sign has issued an order. The garden is musky with rosemary, thyme, oregano; sweet from lavender and loaded apple trees; but the word is a penetration. It was the language of murderers then and of gentle souls now and still, it is chilling. I try to flip it away, but the word shapes inside me, fuses in that biological way, osmosis passing through cell walls, a textbook picture of cell transport—like-it-or-not through membrane. Memory. Membrane. Memory:

Tiferet

Renee Plonski lives across the fence. In our backyard in Cleveland, we bob for marshmallows at every birthday party, our hands behind our backs while we try to bite the bouncing marshmallow hung from the clothesline.

Beyond the clothesline, hidden in creepy shrubs is a rusted chain-link fence, and on the other side, the Plonskis. Renee's father shows up in an undershirt, the corrugated type, skin-tight and muscle style, his stocky frame, his bronzed skin, his never-smiling face. But what I notice at the time and frightens me for reasons I cannot understand, is the inked numbers, the row of them on his forearm, on the tender inner skin—numbers amidst the veins, blurry and terrible for no reason. My mother has died and my body knows terrible.

This terrible is different.

3.
My husband's plate is full. I see why. I stand at the shiny silver hot box; steam pours from its contents as I cautiously lift the lid. Within it, this bounty of cauliflower laced with breadcrumbs, buttery, and the cauliflower tender and hot. This is food my British husband cooks at home in Maryland, and they have served it to us here at the health clinic in Germany. This is the food of his childhood; the food his mother made.

His German mother.

I am elated at yet another discovery of overlap. The day before, we were invited to pick wild herbs with the cook and then watch how she uses them. Borage leaves with their starry blue flowers are chopped with nettle leaves, ribleaf plantago (lamb's tongue), and mint, then gently simmered in water for a light summer soup. Lion's mane mushrooms (bearded hedgehog), with its potential of dementia- and cancer-fighting properties, is a fluffy fungus the cook flattens like a pancake, then dips in egg and breadcrumbs flecked with oregano, salt, baby dandelion, before sautéing in safflower oil and more sprigs of borage.

Now, at dinner, the surprising rock-piles of cauliflower laced with breadcrumbs, a shocking throwback to my mother-in-law's cooking. This is not the stamp of her cordon-bleu training as we'd assumed; this is heritage. This is German food she passed forward—the nettles she hunted in Germany and then London's woods, returning home to make nettle soup for her sons with a loud So! and a proud

116

serving—only to be disappointed by the children's English-bred refusal to taste a soup made from leaves that could sting. This was her German childhood shining through! Like her potato salad. Like her beets. Like her parsnips. All these they serve to us at the vegetarian dining hall of the clinic. I stand before the cauliflower laced with breadcrumbs and am overwhelmed, the desire to shout and call all the quiet eaters forward to see—even those from Kuwait draped in clothes so only eyes show, even those from Switzerland and from Italy—*Come! See my husband's source of knowing!* Cauliflower with breadcrumbs, the comfort food of his childhood.

Ursula, the cook, comes by to replenish the plate of vegan salamis. I call her to the steam tray. I am grinning: "My husband cooks this! His mother cooked it for him! His mother was German!"

His mother was German, I say. I am stating the great equalizer. German. Like you. German like Germany, like this clinic, like the doctors, like the nurses and physical therapists and lymph-drainage therapists, and the lab team and administrative staff—Stefan, Ulf, and Helga.

Later, I recall that our conversation ended only with her smile. Ended with my declaration that his mother was German. To which Ursula smiled and said no other words, nor asked any other question.

4.

At age 13, my future mother-in-law, Malli, is sitting at the piano in the living room of the upstairs apartment in Duisburg, near the draped windows. A shot rings out, breaks through the tall windows and misses her. Uniformed "brownshirts" had been occupying the streets and harassing Jews already, smashing picture windows of her parents' furniture store below. That night, her parents pack a few valuables and leave, in the dark. Leave. Three children left behind.

Exactly what happens next is not clear. Weeks or months after their parents' escape, Malli, with her younger sister and toddler brother, are guided by a hired Dutch citizen to a train to Holland to unite with the parents. Pre-teen Malli is the adult in charge; she pushes her siblings' heads down as the conductor passes, terrified their identities will be questioned.

Tiferet

5.

We are on a train through countryside and towns. The train is clean, no conductor passes through to collect tickets. Every train is on time. History casts a horrific shadow of sealed boxcars stuffed with frightened prisoners; torturous airless travel that was the easy part as they were transported to Hell. Yet, here high school kids board with backpacks, some with bicycles, and seem the usual variety of boisterous, playful, contemporary, shy, and concave.

The land becomes green and beautiful. Terraced grape plants grow on steep, straight-up hills to one side, and a river shines brown and full on the other. Hills are lush, houses are sturdy. A few buildings have murals of graffiti along the train route side. Roofs on modest homes are checkered with solar panels.

The country is thriving, the country feels *responsible*. They are ground creatures, weighted, and a sense of earth, not sea or sky, pervades. Angela Merkel might be under duress and show signs of the same malady as mine—or worse, her tremors might or might not be benign—but of all current leaders she is one of few who I admire: her attempts to bridge the people of her re-united country, to rectify their history's stench, to show compassion to refugees and meld them into German society—surely this is the exact opposite of the minority elimination of Hitler's day. I admire how the woman stands before her country with strength and empathy, vulnerable to mudslinging, poison darts, and terror, even now as the far-right rises. How does a nation undo its past? How do they remember but not mire in it? How do they clean where every bone was rid, where every small footprint was covered with sand? How do they move forward with full due to the innocent next generation yet pull the carcass of their past, that burden that should not lift quickly, that should be renounced again and again?

Since 1952, Germany has paid more than $80 billion in reparations to Holocaust survivors. My grandma-in-law, Ima, lived in England on payments from the German government until she died.

6.

I was raised in the McCarthy era. The FBI came to our door; the files on both my father and my mother were hundreds of pages collected over a decade. On page 7, the FBI agent—posing as a mimeograph machine repairman as he swept around the D.C. Progressive Party office in Dupont Circle—recorded plans for their upcoming fundraiser to be headlined by baritone Paul Robeson. My father, present that day, was an activist college kid. Glued onto page 19 of 400 pages of FBI file, was a postcard another agent later stole after rifling through our family's trash—only proof, it seems, that my grandfather Bill wanted to say hi from Brooklyn. Both of my parents were called to testify before the Senate House Un-American Activities Committee, grilled and probed to name names when Julius and Ethel Rosenberg were accused of sharing atomic secrets and ultimately executed. It was a U.S. extension of antisemitic Nazi Germany and our own near-loss of two parents—closest friends of ours were jailed. Many HUAC accused were both Jews and activists; many of them were artists. My parents were in the perfect storm, and even in 1967, when we moved from Cleveland to Berkeley, the front page of the Berkeley Gazette greeted us as we came home from our first day of elementary school: *Communist Comes to Berkeley.*

7.

When I am assaulted by police in the alley of our backyard, I am 60. The police are eventually found to be wrong, including their lie that I assaulted them, but a potential jail sentence hangs over me for six weeks after I am released from a night of handcuffs and a shared cell.

It is a dark night with men and women in uniform. Fear; powerlessness; the airless drive, handcuffed and locked in a speeding vehicle going to an unknown location in the dark with an angry cop; thumbprints, mugshots, the cold of jail. While I write this, my husband enters the room to get something, and as he turns the knob, a bag I'd hung on the conjoining knob falls to the floor and the bang of plastic bottles waiting for recycle is explosive. I jump and scream. Such is the ongoing edginess of this multi-sensory topic: *the banging jail cell door. The lock.*

While in the cell, a sudden re-play occurs in my head—of words that slipped from my mouth as two cops jumped me. Later, the proof is in a low-tech recording from my son's videotaping, youth's use of cell phone that proves invaluable both for freeing his mom from criminal charges, and for the phrase it confirms I spoke:

"For crying out loud," I said, two cops on my back. "I'm just trying to walk to my son."

For crying out loud is not a phrase I say; this is not my style of speech even at the most irritated moments of indignation. It is a phrase my father said, however, when

he had really had it, when the "arc of the moral universe" had tired him and some
thing, possibly some insignificant thing, had put him over the top. It came out of
unuttered storage stuffed in the language-hut of my chest. Or my belly. It rose from
my gut the way a French poem about a puppet rose when I once drove into Quebec,
though I hadn't uttered that poem since first grade. These digestions, those herbs,
that cauliflower, these words—even at the clinic when I participated in the gentle
yet oddly disturbing marching in place led by a physical therapist in noon-time
exercise—all of these quiet links are the stunning knowledge of history's dropbox,
stored in the generation that is returning to the earth, and the generation that carries
on. Like radiation, it remains, though filtered, fainter. There is "nothing" actual to
remember; I wasn't there—we weren't there. Yet we remember, we do remember. We
frighteningly remember. I check with my sisters because I hear German phrases in
my mind that have no outlined spelling, only their rhythm, set and real. *Du dummes
schwein hunt* is one we call up— *you stupid pig hunt*. The thread, I don't know.
But the deliverer was my father, the son of American-born parents. He learned
odd German phrases overseas in the war, a war of which he later refused to speak.
These phrases roll through my head and the rhythms stick to my tongue. I want to
google-translate them, but my rendition is too far-fetched to spell. I don't dare try
these pigeon phrases on the Germans around me, and we don't mention my father's
service in the war. We don't mention my mother-in-law again after the cauliflower
excitement, and we don't happen to mention to anyone, as my blood is drawn and
veins infused with micro-nutrients, that although I was not educated as such, and
although my second mother was Baptist and Grandpa Bill became a Christian
Scientist, by birth both my husband and I are Jewish.

8.
I may be trembling less. My husband and I begin to notice this at dinner. Tremors
began about seven years ago, but no big deal, they were slight, and I was assured by a
neurologist that they were benign tremors, not Parkinson's. The police assault didn't
help, adrenaline and cortisol baited them further. I remember guards taking me from
the cell in handcuffs at 2 a.m. for a second set of thumbprints, the first ones too
fuzzy I was shaking so.

One cause of neurological disorders such as trembling is metal toxicity. Suspected
is mercury—perhaps from the incomplete removal of amalgam fillings. I'm no
expert, but remnant flecks seem potentially more active than whole metal left alone.
My osteopath in Maryland had been to clinics in both California and Germany
for heavy metal removal—chelation, it's called—and when I knew I was flying to

Europe anyway, it was time. I didn't trust my local American holistic doctors, and to see them for extensive treatment we would've had to mortgage our little house. The German clinic staff of "Original Christians" believe in the Ten Commandments of Moses as criteria for daily life, and promote unity of all people, harmonious with animals and nature. My room was 40 euros a night with great vegetarian food. Sure enough, my lab reports showed mercury levels ten times the point of "tolerance." I had three sets of infusion treatments and was advised to return.

9.

Esther Perel is a sex therapist. The author of *State of Affairs: Rethinking Infidelity,* Perel normalizes complicated issues of marriage and sex. In an NPR interview two years ago, I was astounded by her belief in the ultimate transformation of a relationship after betrayal:

There will be post-traumatic stress—and [then] there may be post-traumatic growth.

The interview helped me remain social with our friend George, who betrayed his (now ex-) wife with a 2-year secretive marital affair. Renewal is what Perel perceives possible even after the worst transgression. She has vision that scopes beyond the obvious single hue, to the polychromatic color that is white light. Marriage is complex, and even betrayal is a dance between two people and their history. I look up Esther Perel, and am most surprised to see the life-teaching that set her on this path, the ultimate transcendence beyond any I have lived, the one I've always wondered could I overcome:

> *My parents Sala Ferlegier and Icek Perel were survivors of the Nazi concentration camps and sole survivors of their respective families. My father had nine siblings, my mother, seven. For four years, my parents stood face to face with death. Trauma was woven into the fabric of my family history (and would inspire my work for years to come). They came out of that experience wanting to charge at life with a vengeance and to make the most of each day. They both felt that they had been granted a unique gift: living life again. My parents didn't just want to survive, they wanted to revive. They wanted to embrace vibrancy and vitality — in the mystical sense of the word, the erotic. I owe them much of my perspective on life, as well as my belief in the power of will, the search for meaning, and the resilience of the human spirit. To me, there is a world of difference between "not being dead" and "being alive". I owe this understanding to my parents.*

Tiferet

10.
I will return to Germany for another round of chelation therapy.

There exists an admittedly painful desire to transcend horror, to polychromatize what is singular, the very accent you find ugly, the very people you've held in fear; to know and digest the horrific betrayals to human morality and yet, in Perel's words, *not just survive but revive.*

When I finish writing my book for assault survivors, we will fly back to Germany and return to the clinic. Trains will take us again from the airport to the closest town.

German teens will hop on with their backpacks, some with bikes, some chatting and laughing, some on phones or staring out windows. Innocent in their bodies, which are light and seemingly unburdened as if their toxic history is less potent upon them than their parents, they'll jump on and off the train with ease. They remind me of my younger son, who comfortably tells people he is Jewish. On a Maryland high school soccer field, when the captain shouted across the green, *Hey, look, our whole team is Hispanic!* my son raised his hand and shouted, *Hey! Actually? I'm Jewish.* I, on the other hand, will not reveal myself at the clinic, where they beautifully pronounce my Hungarian name, a kind of grape, a kind of wine, a region of Hungary in which no Jews remain. I will offer my veined forearm to the kind nurse, though, and thank her as she helps de-toxify what makes me shake.

FICTION

The History Lesson

Murzban F. Shroff

Anuradha Singhal (Anu hereafter) stepped out of the Chhatrapati Shivaji International Airport and combed the faces at the exit. He would be easy to spot: her Jai. Not because he was six feet two inches in shoes but because he was her darling man, the undisputed owner of her heart, father to the warm bundle of joy she held in her arms and who was now asleep: thank God, for that! The flight from Dubai had not been easy. Although they had traveled business-class, it had made baby cranky. She had cried for over an hour, much to the discomfort of other passengers.

The flight attendant – a fair, stocky, wide-hipped woman in her late thir-ties - hadn't been much help. Anu thought she looked the kind who saw her job as a chore. The excitement of flying had long dried in her face. You could see she had been through it all: the thrills of sightseeing, the frenzy of shopping, the joys of tasting multiple cuisines and wines. She would have furnished her home with the latest gadgets, and bought expensive gifts for her family. She would have been on disaster-dates with pursers and fought off advances from same–sex colleagues, with whom she would have shared a room. She would have received her share of proposi-tions from drunken passengers, for whom she would have felt nothing but pity; and she would have known heartbreak, searing, wincing heartbreak, in her trysts with the dashing, unwilling-to-commit pilots. And that heartbreak would have changed her. It would explain to Anu why she now wore a sullen look, the makeup failing to hide the disappointment. It would also explain to Anu why this heavy-shouldered, wing-less angel in the sky would shove so roughly a rubber nipple under baby's chin, say-ing: "Here, take this, and be quiet!" There was no kindness in that tone, no profes-sional courtesy either, and first it angered Anu, and then it saddened her, saddened her that baby would have to grope her way around in this unfeeling world of service attendants and poseurs.

But right now there was the joy of home! Dirty, filthy Mumbai, with its ve-neer of slums, rushing to meet the slow-descending aircraft, had the power to stir her heart. It did not matter what the city looked like from the sky. Something in it had the tendency to raise in her a leaping excitement. She felt like this after every single vacation. Felt excited beyond words.

Tiferet

Now, wheeling the bags' trolley with one hand, baby in the other, Anu sallied forth, a slim, elegant figure in a trouser-suit.

"Oh, Trimbuksh!" she called to Jai's chauffeur, who was craning his neck to be seen above the swarm of faces and, as though spurred by her presence, Trimbuksh indicated to her with a motion of his fingers that he'd get the car, she should wait there. He shuffled his way toward the parking lot, a bulky, anxious figure in his forties, wearing a starched white uniform and a stiff white cap.

"Hotel, madam?" a tout at Anu's elbow offered. "Very nice. Very comfortable. Close by! And safe for baby."

"No thank-you," said Anu. "I am from Mumbai. I reside here." Her fingers tightened around the trolley handle and her eyes fixed onto the bags. One, two, three, four … yes, all there!

The car swept in. Jai's Audi. Sleek as a panther, dark as the night.

Anu strained her eyes to see past the tinted windows. Could it be possible? she wondered. But, no, he wasn't there.

Trimbuksh sprang from the driver's seat. With thick, brawny arms, he heaved the luggage from the trolley into the trunk of the car. He knew which suitcase should go on top and which at the bottom. Baby's hamper, he placed upfront, on the seat next to him. Then he opened wide the door for Anu, so that she could slide in without disturbing baby.

The car slid over the overpass, and Anu breathed a sigh of relief. This was home. The cool comfort of the car. The enveloping softness of the seats. The familiar back of Trimbuksh. The neon lights frozen bright, as though to welcome her home.

Glancing at her in the rear-view mirror, Trimbuksh spoke. "How are Pratap Sahib and Roma Memsahib?" he asked. "They must have been thrilled to see baby, no."

"They are fine," Anu said. "Sahib hardly went to work while we were there, and memsahib had friends over daily, to see baby. They will be coming to Mumbai more often now. What we haven't been able to do in years this little one has achieved without a word."

"A child changes things, madam. It can change the toughest human beings. I know how my parents were when Karambuksh was born. They took hundreds of photographs of him and couldn't stop boasting to all the neighbors. Of course, my parents were excited because it was a boy. In our community we believe that if the first child is a boy, then God is pleased with you."

"Tell me about Jai Sahib," said Anu sharply. "Has he been working late? Taking his meals on time? Going for his yoga workouts?" She glanced at baby sleeping in angelic composure.

124

"Madam, you know sahib. His work is his life. Meetings and more meetings! That is all he has been doing since you went. It is good that you are back. Now he will come home early."

Anu suppressed a sigh. That man of hers was incapable of looking after himself. And to think he had promised her he would. This was just before she had entered the departure lounge and the doors had closed behind her. There was no point pressing Trimbuksh for details, which she could use to chide Jai. Trimbuksh was fiercely loyal to his boss. He had known Jai since Jai was a boy. He had seen Jai through his feisty pub-hopping days, which Anu had heard about from Jai's friends. She had also heard about his numerous girlfriends, who clung to his every word, aspired to his bed, and to whom Jai would commit no more than a few nights of pleasure.

"He was a real a hound in heat till he met you," a friend of Jai once told her.

"He still is!" she had replied. "Only more focused," she had laughed.

Now she couldn't imagine Jai like that. There was nothing of the rake left in him. He was, instead, the closest thing to an ideal husband. Sweet, lovable Jai! Always so caring, so sweet! Anu could hug Fate for what it had delivered to her.

Initially, she had some doubts about their relationship. She would wonder if they would survive the differences in their backgrounds – he from a family of affluent builders, she from a middle-class family. Her father was a doctor with a small private practice; her mother was a teacher. There was never any scarcity, but no abundance, either. From an early age, she was taught to respect money, to understand the value of every rupee spent. But, here, in her marital home, huge amounts were discussed with nonchalance. The figures would send her mind reeling.

A ring!

At last! she thought, fumbling in her handbag.

"Darling!" said the voice at the other end. "Where are you?"

"We have just left the airport. Are on the highway. But why aren't you here? Kiyomi is sleeping right now, but she gave me a frightful time on the flight. Bawled throughout. It was our good luck that no one complained."

"Something must have disturbed her. It must have been too cold. Or maybe her ears were blocked."

"Darling, I love your faith in your daughter, but you must accept there are times when she can be a perfect terror. For no other reason than the fact that she *is* one."

Tiferet

"As long as she is fine now," said Jai, doubtfully. "I am with the Americans. I excused myself from the table. To call you."

"Will you be late?" she asked.

"I think so. They have big plans for India and want us in with them. Us, out of all the builders in this country. Listen, sweetheart, is all well with you? I need to return to the table. I just wanted to hear your voice and know that Ki is fine."

"Yes, all good. But *where* are you? You didn't say." Her heart was heavy with longing. She couldn't bear this distance now that she knew she was *that* close to him, that he was available to her in the same city. Those fifteen days in Dubai had seemed like a lifetime, an ordeal. All she wanted to do was slip into her husband's arms and snuggle up.

"We are at The Rooftop."

"Ok, I won't hold you then. Take care and see you soon. And good luck with the Americans. Tell them that my man *is* the best. They needn't look beyond."

"Love you, precious," he said, and hung up.

She dropped the phone into her handbag and leaned her head against the headrest. Suddenly she felt tired. She felt her body go limp. She should sleep, she thought. She could now afford to.

The car raced along the road, which was full of bumps and potholes, but she did not feel them. The Audi was clearly a superior vehicle. And Trimbuksh *was* the expert handler. Trimbuksh *was* the man at the wheel. He could be trusted: Anu knew that, Jai knew that. Which explained why Jai, from all his drivers, had chosen to send Trimbuksh to receive his darling wife and child. His family was in safe hands. And they were being returned to him. Now he could focus on the business at hand. Business which could not wait.

As he sat down, the fat American at his table leaned forward and said, "You see, Mr. Singhal, the way we see it, there are only three things permanent in the world: the sun, the moon, and America. And what we want you to understand is that America is ready to invest in India and in you. We like you, Mr. Singhal. More than any of the other builders we have met so far. You've got style, you've got taste, *and* you've got history, which is the most important thing of all. History is what the others don't have. And America is a country that respects history. It respects lineage in a company. Because lineage means you are here to stay. You are here to deliver continuity. Which is why we admire you. Now, let me tell you one thing, Mr. Singhal, strictly between you and me. Whoever comes in with us is going to be the next Olly Baba. He is going to walk away with a fortune."

Olly Baba? Oh, he meant Ali Baba from the book *Arabian Nights,* who had stumbled onto a cave of treasures belonging to a band of thieves. He said, "Well, gentlemen, let me assure you, I am equally excited about your plans. I don't know about being the next Ali Baba; Singhal Constructions is doing well enough for itself. But to create American-style cities in India, to build a new India: that would be any builder's dream."

The second American spoke. He was older, more cautious, with a pock-marked face and silver-rimmed glasses. "Timing is everything, Mr. Singhal," he said. "The way things are right now, we have investors interested in India. And India, we know, is interested in building smart cities. So we need to work fast. We need to get Delhi involved in this. Which is where you come in. With your contacts and reputation. Once we have created an American-style infrastructure here, we will back you in every way. We will show you how to make it profitable and sustainable. You should know one thing about America: we never let down our friends."

"I am aware of that, gentlemen," said Jai, reaching for his glass and raising it. "To two of the greatest democracies in the world and their partnership! What can we not achieve with a shared wavelength and a shared vision?" The word "values" rose in his throat, but for some reason he swallowed it.

Sipping his whiskey, Jai felt pleased with himself. In school he had suffered from stage fright. But now he was eloquence itself. Must be the whiskey, he thought. It was making him glib, giving him ideas. He was already thinking where the new cities should be built. Along the coast. Coast to coast. Yes, Indians loved beaches. They loved the water. Any place where they could dip their feet without getting their bodies wet. That's why the hill cities had failed. Indians hated isolation, seclusion. And the hills isolated them. Besides, there was a lengthy coastline just waiting to be tapped. The fisherfolk could be rehabilitated. He would make them stakeholders in the new cities. Give them a share of the net profits. Look at Alibaug, Kihim, Mandva, and Goa: how these places had boomed. Were still booming. But, God, where was his family? Where had they reached? He was missing them like crazy. Especially Ki. That daughter of his was something. She had played hell into her co-passengers. Well, she was a princess, and royalty does just that: it makes its presence felt.

The third American leaned forward. He was young, slim, bald, blue-eyed, and clean-shaven. To Jai's mind, he looked like a robot, a carefully constructed robot, perfectly sculpted and gleaming all over. He said, "We have thought through everything. Yes, everything. We will get professional companies to do the research. If it's music people want, we will give them a city with music. A Memphis, a Nashville, or a San Francisco. If it's entertainment they want, we will recreate L.A. If it's architecture, we will rebuild Chicago. If it's art and fashion, we will replicate New York. And if they want eco-friendly, we will do Portland. That's how we will bring America to India." He smiled at Jai through thin lips, without opening his mouth, without showing any teeth, and it made Jai shiver. It made him wonder: it all sounded so simple, but what was in it for them?

The American continued, "Of course, we will create American-style offices and make American products. We will set up American universities and American malls. We will replicate the whole American system here. So what you get, in effect, is the infrastructure, knowledge, and expertise of a superpower."

He paused and looked at Jai expectantly. They all did. They were expecting him to say something. To express surprise, pleasure, even gratitude. But all he could manage was a nod.

The fat guy reached for a paper roll at his feet and spread it out on the table. Jai was surprised: a map of Mumbai. Holding it down with a pudgy palm, the fat man pointed to the east side, where there were saltpans, mangroves, and oil refineries. "This is a part of Mumbai we could exploit," he said. "We could develop a township here. A model township, which could become the norm, the gold standard. We could set up offices, malls, parks, cinema houses, gated communities, a high-tech hospital, international schools, colleges, a university. There is enough land, I am told. Well over 5000 acres." Wow, thought Jai, these guys were prepared. They had come prepared to do business, to move in.

Now, for some strange reason, he remembered a history lesson from school. It came to him like a wave out of nowhere, and he submitted to the memory, because it filled him with a sweet euphoria, a sensation like honey pouring onto an outstretched tongue.

It was the start of a new academic year. He was in grade six, still in half pants. The Jesuit priest, Father Fredrick Noronha, had walked into the classroom, drawn the map of India on the blackboard, and said, "Boys, *this* is your country. A beautiful woman, a hauntingly beautiful woman, surrounded by hostile neighbors. There will be some countries that will lust after her from a distance and be content with that. But there will be others who will want to possess her, change her, even steal her beauty." And then he had gone on to explain how it had always been that way. Century after century, they had invaded India. First the Moguls. Then the Dutch. Then the Portuguese. Then the French. And, finally, the British. For seven hundred years, the invaders had feasted on India's beauty; they had bled her dry. But now, she must rise on her own strengths. Because she had been set free by the bravest of souls. They who cared neither for their lives nor for their careers. Nor for any of the fame their struggles brought them.

Jai looked at the delegation before him. They were smiling, waiting for his answer. Waiting for him to say something. Anything that would further their plans and their relationship, that would reassure them that the meeting had paid off.

"Gentlemen," he said. "I don't think you have been correctly informed. The landmass you speak of is the water catchment area of the city; it is our green cover against floods. The land that is being considered for development is barely a thousand acres. Which would make no sense to you as a business investment. No sense at all. Besides, you would do well to remember that this is saltpan land and the soil here has been greatly weakened by the continuous production of salt. This means whoever builds here will have to drill very deep, till they hit bedrock. Which means your cost of construction is going to be extremely high and not without risks. Now, gentlemen -" he rose to his feet. "If you will excuse me, my family is on its way back from the airport, and I must be home to receive them. I haven't seen them since what - two weeks! Which is way too long for a family man such as me. The restaurant staff has been instructed to look after you. Please eat and drink to your heart's content. Feel free to order anything you want. I am traveling from tomorrow, but will discuss your ideas with my board, on my return. You will appreciate that something as big as the creation of a city will need the approval of the board. I am unable to commit to it on my own. Meanwhile, I thank you for considering us and for giving us so much importance. I am sure that we will always be friends, good friends, and that you can count on our hospitality whenever you visit India." With that, he bowed and walked away swiftly, feeling like a king who had protected his kingdom. Feeling lighter and more powerful, somehow.

The first thing he did when he got into his car was to call his wife, his darling wife. She would be pleased to know he was on his way back.

But she did not pick up her phone. It just rang and rang and rang.

And then he called up Trimbuksh, who responded right away. "Yes, sir. Madam is here. But she couldn't hear the phone because we are stuck in a procession. There is too much noise, and they are diverting all the traffic. No idea, sir, when we will reach. Yes, baby is awake, wide, wide awake, and watching. No, she is not scared. In fact, she is very much enjoying the music." In the background, Jai could hear shouts, screams, drums, a keyboard wailing, and trumpets blaring.

Trimbuksh gave the phone to Anu, who rubbed it a couple of times against her trouser before bringing it to her ear. "Darling," she said. "This is madness! Sheer madness! It is not even the festive season and they are out on the streets, dancing and bursting crackers. No, I have no idea what they are celebrating, and Trimbuksh doesn't know, either. Seems like some local event. They have taken over the entire road, and the cops are doing nothing about it. I am sorry, darling, but we are going to be late. I can't say how late. You know how these processions are."

And of course Jai knew. He knew well enough for him to chuckle at himself, of a few minutes ago, sitting at the city's most premium restaurant and planning the future of the country. To think that you could build an American-style city in India; to think that you could change the culture of this country; to think that you could stop a five-thousand-year-old civilization from pouring out into the street and expressing itself: that was sheer impudence, sheer delusion.

He swung his car onto Marine Drive. The seafront stretched before him like a giant smile, a dazzling, winking smile that seemed to say: I know what can never be corrupted in this city. I know what will *always* heal and refresh.

God, thought Jai, how he loved this city! This space-squeezed city that had no option but to go vertical. Sometimes he felt like a predator, looking for spaces to build: a slum, a defunct mill, a municipal compound, a public garden. Then getting permissions by paying off politicians, bureaucrats, and civic officials. The worst were the slumlords, who cleared the decks for him. He had to visit them, eat with them, attend their daughters' marriages, provide employment to their sons and nephews. What a life! he thought, that it trapped you in unholy alliances, forced you to work with people you dislike. He wondered if it would have been the same working with the Americans. Would he have to swallow his pride? Play ball? Compromise? Here, at least, he was feeding the domestic demand for survival. He was giving back to his own people, hoping that one day their stomachs would be full.

A bus hooted at his rear and promptly he gave way, darting to one side, then slipping into the slow lane. Fumbling in his glove compartment, he pulled out a CD and slipped it into the player. Then, as the familiar song came on, he drummed on the steering wheel and hummed: *I'm an alien, I'm a legal alien; I'm an Englishman in New York.*

 Contributors

DOUG ANDERSON

Doug Anderson's first book of poems, *The Moon Reflected Fire,* from Alice James Books, won the Kate Tufts Discovery Award, and his second, *Blues for Unemployed Secret Police,* a grant from the Academy of American Poets. His memoir, *Keep Your Head Down,* was published by W.W. Norton in 2009. His most recent book of poems is *Horse Medicine,* from Barrow Street Books. He has also written plays, film scripts, journalism and fiction. His play, *Short Timers,* was produced at Theater for the New City in New York. His work has appeared in Ploughshares, the Southern Review, Poetry, Field, the Massachusetts Review, the Virginia Quarterly Review and many other journals and magazines. His grants and awards include a fellowship from the National Endowment for the Arts, the Massachusetts Cultural Council, Poets & Writers, the Virginia Quarterly Review, and other funding organizations. He teaches in the MFA Program at Western New England University.

RENÉE ASHLEY

Renée Ashley is also the author of a novel and six previous volumes of poetry: most recently, *The View from the Body* (Black Lawrence Press) and *Because I Am the Shore I Want To Be the Sea* (Subito Book Prize, University of Colorado—Boulder). She has received fellowships in both poetry and prose from the NJSCA and a fellowship in poetry from the NEA. She's on the faculty of Fairleigh Dickinson University's MFA in Creative Writing and the MA in Creative Writing and Literature for Educators. Her new collection of poetry, *Ruined Traveler,* will be published in autumn 2019.

JENNIFER BARBER

Jennifer Barber's books are *Works on Paper* (Word Works, Tenth Gate Prize, published in 2016), *Given Away* (Kore Press, 2012), and *Rigging the Wind* (Kore Press, 2003). The founding editor of *Salamander,* she was the 2017 Isabella Gardner Fellow at the MacDowell Colony. Recent poems appear in *Upstreet* and *December.*

PHYLLIS BARBER

Phyllis Barber has published eight books, including the prize-winning memoir, *How I Got Cultured*. A ninth book, a historical novel titled *The Camel and the Third Wife,* is due out in Spring 2020. Barber has been inducted into the Nevada Writers Hall of Fame, has received many awards for her fiction, memoirs, and essays, and has an affection for long-necked animals.

Tiferet

ANGELA BEAN

Angela Bean is a certified immigration lawyer in California specializing in deportation defense, family visas and complex naturalization cases. *Unaccompanied Minors* was inspired by her recent volunteer work on the Texas border with Central American adolescent boys placed in involuntary foster care. She lives in Oakland, California.

MIRIAM BERKLEY

Miriam Berkley published widely as a journalist specializing in books and publishing before turning to photography full time. Her photographs of writers have appeared in print and other media worldwide, earning her a significant reputation. The portrait photographer for the Sewanee Writers Conference since its inception, she also exhibits and sells images of her hometown of New York City. The publication of "Path," written over 40 years ago but kept in a drawer ever since, marks Berkley's return to her earliest love, poetry.

LAURA BOSS

Laura Boss is a first prize winner of PSA's Gordon Barber Poetry Contest. She is a recipient of three NJSCA Fellowships. Founder and Editor of Lips, recent books include *Arms: New and Selected Poems; Flashlight* (both Guernica Editions); and *The Best Lover* (NYQ). A Dodge Poet, her poems have appeared in *The New York Times.*

MICHELLE CAMERON

Michelle Cameron is the author of the forthcoming historical novel, *Beyond the Ghetto Gates* (April 2020), set during Napoleon's Italian campaign, and now available for pre-order. Her novel, *The Fruit of Her Hands* (2009) was based on the life of her thirteenth-century ancestor, and her full-length novel in verse, *In the Shadow of the Globe* (2003) was the Shakespeare Theatre of NJ's 2003-4 Winter Book Selection. Michelle is a director of The Writers Circle which offers creative writing to children, teens, and adults in five NJ locations. Her website is michelle-cameron.com.

JUDITH A. CHRISTIAN

Poet and artist Judith A. Christian has been a Pushcart Prize nominee and former president of South Mountain Poets. She was instrumental in the editing and production of several South Mountain anthologies of New Jersey poets. Her book, *A Certain Knowing,* was published by The Paulinskill Poetry Project in 2018.

ELIZABETH COHEN

Elizabeth Cohen is an associate professor of English at Plattsburgh State University in New York and editor of *Saranac Review*. She is the author of *The Family on Beartown Road*, a memoir, *the Hypothetical Girl*, short stories, and five books of poetry, including *The Patron Saint of Cauliflower*, out this summer from Saint Julian Press.

JAMES CREWS

Recent work appears in *Ploughshares, The New Republic, Christian Century* and *Poet Lore*, among other journals. James is the author of two collections of poetry, *The Book of What Stays* (Prairie Schooner Prize, 2011) and *Telling my Father* (Cowles Prize, 2017) and the editor of *Healing the Divide: Poems of Kindness and Connection* (Green Writers Press, 2019).

LYNN DOMINA

Lynn Domina is the author of two collections of poetry, *Corporal Works* and *Framed in Silence*, and the editor of a collection of essays, *Poets on the Psalms*. She is creative writing editor of *The Other Journal* and serves as Head of the English Department at Northern Michigan University. Read more here: www.lynndomina.com.

CATHERINE DOTY

Catherine Doty is the author of *Momentum*, a volume of poems from CavanKerry Press. She is the recipient of a fellowship from the National Endowment for the Arts, as well as an Academy of American Poets Prize and fellowships from The New Jersey State Council on the Arts and the New York Foundation for the Arts.

JANE EBIHARA

Jane Ebihara is a retired teacher living in Allamuchy, NJ. She is the author of two poetry collections, *A Little Piece of Mourning* and *A Reminder of Hunger and Wings* (both from Finishing Line Press). She is the recipient of a fellowship to the Fine Arts Work Center in Provincetown, MA, and her poems have appeared in various journals and anthologies, including *Adanna, Tiferet, U.S. 1 Worksheets*, and *The Stillwater Review*.

JAMY & PETER FAUST

Jamy and Peter Faust have been facilitating Family Constellations in their Immersion Program, Seminars and private practices since 2002. They are the authors of *The Constellation Approach: Finding Peace Through Your Family Lineage* and *Poems of Love, Sex and God*. Jamy is a psychotherapist, energy healer, and shamanic practitioner. Peter is an acupuncturist, energy healer and men's work facilitator. They have worked alongside each other to support the evolution of consciousness for over thirty years.

ILONA FRIED

Ilona Fried is a traveler at heart and finds that new environments reveal aspects of the self that might otherwise remain concealed. Her personal blog and links to other published essays can be found at www.ilonafried.com.

PAUL GENEGA

Paul Genega's sixth collection of poetry, *Sculling on the Lethe*, was published by Salmon Poetry in 2018. Over a long career, his work has received numerous awards, including an individual fellowship from the National Endowment for the Arts. His poetry has also been included in the play *Ophelia Comes to Brooklyn* and in the multimedia performance piece *Paging Doctor Faustus*, which he is creating with composer/filmmaker Patricia Lee Stotter.

MARIA GIURA

Maria Giura, PhD, is the author of the newly published *Celibate: A Memoir* (Apprentice House Press) about her struggle to hang onto her faith in the midst of trying to understand--and untangle herself from--her complex relationship with a Catholic priest. She is also the author of *What My Father Taught Me* (Bordighera Press 2018), a finalist for the Paterson Poetry Book Prize. Her writing has also appeared in *Prime Number, Presence, VIA, Italian Americana,* and *Lips.* She has won awards from the Academy of American Poets and the Center for Women Writers and has taught Literature and Writing at multiple universities.

MARY GRIMM

Mary Grimm has had two books published, *Left to Themselves* (novel) and *Stealing Time* (story collection) - both by Random House. Currently, she is working on a dystopian novel about oldsters. She teaches fiction writing at Case Western Reserve University.

JUDITH HARRIS

Judith Harris is the author of three books of poetry (LSU), *Night Garden, The Bad Secret, Atonement* and a critical book, *Signifying Pain.* Her poetry has appeared in *The Hudson Review, The Nation, The Atlantic, The New Republic, Slate, The New York Times, Ploughshares, Boulevard, The Southern Review* and *American Life in Poetry.*

MARK HILLRINGHOUSE

Mark Hillringhouse has published photographs, essays, and poetry in many books, anthologies, magazines and journals. His most recent publication is *Paterson Light and Shadow*, from Serving House Press, a book of his black and white Paterson photographs published alongside Maria Mazziotti Gillan's Paterson poems.

TERESA H. JANSSEN

Teresa H. Janssen has received the Norman Mailer/NCTE nonfiction award and was a finalist in Bellingham Review's Annie Dillard nonfiction contest. Her writing has appeared in *Anchor Magazine, Zyzzyva*, and *Lunch Ticket* among other publications. Teresa is at work on an essay collection about a year in Ecuador.

CAROLE JOHANNSEN

Carole Johannsen is an Episcopal priest and a hospital chaplain. For 20 years she has ministered to those whose bodies and minds have the attention of the medical community, but whose spirits cry out for healing as well. She works outside of the institutional church, although a bishop formally endorses her for her work. When patients ask me where my church is, she tells them, "Here, by your bed." There is no religious hierarchy in her "church," no polished brass or silk vestments.

SIHAM KARAMI

Siham Karami's poetry collection *To Love the River* (Kelsay Books, 2018) celebrates life as a spiritual pursuit. Her work is published or forthcoming in *The Orison Anthology, The Comstock Review, Able Muse, Measure, Presence, The Rumpus, Pleiades,* and *Tupelo Quarterly Review*, among others. Currently, she is working on a chapbook of ghazals which was a finalist in two contests. Visit her blog at sihamkarami. wordpress.com.

ROGAN KELLY

Rogan Kelly is a writer and educator. His poems have been featured or are forthcoming in *Bending Genres, Brazenhead Review, The Cortland Review, The Citron Review, The Penn Review, Shrew Literary Zine, Small Orange* and elsewhere. He was a finalist for the 2018 Jane Underwood Poetry Prize. His chapbook, *Demolition in the Tropics*, was published by Seven Kitchens Press.

ADELE KENNY

Adele Kenny has been Tiferet's poetry editor since 2006. She is the author of 24 books. Among other awards, she has received poetry fellowships from the NJ State Arts Council, a Merton Poetry of the Sacred Award, Kean University's Distinguished Alumni Award, and one of her books was a Paterson Poetry Prize finalist. A former creative writing professor, she is founding director of the Carriage House Poetry Series.

Tiferet

ALLEN KESTEN

Allen Kesten is a writer and educator living in Cambridge, Massachusetts. His stories have appeared in *The Sun, Bitter Oleander, Zahir, Maine Review, Mount Hope, The Examined Life*, and other literary magazines. A collection of stories by Allen was a semi-finalist for the 2018 BOA Short Fiction Prize.

FRED LAMOTTE

Fred LaMotte is an interfaith college chaplain and instructor in World Religions who has published two volumes of poems with Saint Julian Press. He lives near Seattle WA with his wife Anna and golden poodle, Willy.

LAURA MARSHALL

Laura Marshall is a New Orleans native currently based in New York City. She has an MFA in creative writing from Hunter College, and her work appears or is forthcoming in *Salon, Reductress, Raleigh Review*, and elsewhere. She resides in Brooklyn with her dog, Max, and her cat, Bowser.

WILLIAM O'DALY

William O'Daly has published nine books of translation of Nobel laureate Pablo Neruda, most recently *Book of Twilight,* a finalist for the 2018 Northern California Book Award. O'Daly's chapbooks of poems include *The Whale in the Web, The Road to Isla Negra, Water Ways* (a collaboration with JS Graustein), and most recently *Yarrow and Smoke.*

JANE O'SHIELDS-HAYNER

Jane O'Shields-Hayner is a writer and visual artist living in the foothills of the Santa Ana Mountains in Southern California. Her work spans the distance between her backyard and the universe, traversing cultural, political and spiritual terrain as she tells the stories of how they blend and bleed into one another. Jane lives with her husband and two of their four children on the edge of a canyon, where wild and domestic creatures coexist. She writes creative non-fiction, fiction and poetry. Her recent work has been published in *Tiferet Journal, Friends Journal, Lady Liberty Lit., The Manifest Station* and *Western Friend.* She is currently completing a trilogy of short-stories written in homage to Kurt Vonnegut, jr.

JULIA PARK TRACEY

Julia Park Tracey was Poet Laureate of Alameda, CA, from 2014-2017. Her poems and poetry reviews have been published most recently in *Sugared Water, Sweatpants & Coffee, East Bay Review, Postcard Poems,* and *Yellow Chair Review.* She is the author of three novels, two women's history compilations and Amaryllis, a collection of poetry. Find her online I/FB/T @juliaparktracey.

KARL PLANK

Karl Plank is the author of *A Field, Part Arable* (Lithic, 2017) and *BOSS: Rewriting Rilke* (Red Bird, 2017). His work has appeared in publications such as *Beloit Poetry Journal, Spiritus,* and *Notre Dame Review,* and has been featured on *Poetry Daily.* He is the J.W. Cannon Professor of Religious Studies at Davidson College.

TOM PLANTE

Tom Plante was born in New York City. He studied Geography at the University of California, Berkeley, and worked for several newspapers, including *The Berkeley Barb, The Irish Echo,* and *The Courier News.* Tom has published the poetry journal *Exit 13 Magazine* since 1988 (Exit13magazine@yahoo.com). His recent collection of poems is *Atlas Apothecary.* His poems have appeared in *Ireland of the Welcomes, Lips,* and *US1 Worksheets.* Tom and his wife live in Fanwood, New Jersey.

SUSAN RICH

Susan Rich is the author of four poetry collections including, *Cloud Pharmacy* and *The Alchemist's Kitchen* (White Pine Press). She also co-edited the travel anthology, *The Strangest of Theatres: Poets Crossing Borders* published by the Poetry Foundation. Rich has received awards from the Fulbright Foundation and The Times Literary Supplement (London). New work appears this year in *Field, New England Review, Pleiades,* and *the Southern Review.*

JACK RIDLE

Jack Ridl, Poet Laureate of Douglas, Michigan (population 783), received the best collection of poetry award from ForeWord Review/Indie Books for *Practicing to Walk Like a Heron,* and The Society of Midland Authors named his *Broken Symmetry* the year's best book of poetry.

JUDE RITTENHOUSE

Jude Rittenhouse is a writer, teacher, speaker, editor, and holistic consultant (Nondual Kabbalistic Healer with a Master's Degree in Counseling). She has received a Writers' Grant from the Vermont Studio Center, poetry awards from Glimmer Train Press and Poets & Patrons of Chicago, and her poems have been finalists multiple times for both the Pablo Neruda Award and the Tiferet Poetry Prize. Her work has been published in many literary magazines and anthologies, including *Nimrod International Journal; Balancing the Tides; River Oak Review;* and *Lay Bare the Canvas: New England Poets on Art,* among others.

JANE ROSENBERG LAFORGE

Jane Rosenberg LaForge lives in New York. She is the author of six volumes of poetry, the newest being *Daphne and Her Discontents* (Ravenna Press). Her novel, *The Hawkman: A Fairy Tale of the Great War* (Amberjack Publishing) was a finalist in the 2019 Eric Hoffer awards. Her memoir is *An Unsuitable Princess* (Jaded Ibis Press). New work has appeared or is forthcoming in *After the Pause, North Dakota Quarterly,* and *The Comstock Review.*

NICHOLAS SAMARAS

Nicholas Samaras' first book, *Hands of the Saddlemaker,* won The Yale Series of Younger Poets Award. His next book, *American Psalm, World Psalm,* came out (2014) from Ashland Poetry Press. Individual poems have appeared or are forthcoming in *The New Yorker, Poetry, New York Times,* etc.

MURZBAN F. SHROFF

Murzban F. Shroff is the author of *Breathless in Bombay* (stories), *Waiting for Jonathan Koshy* (novel) and *Fasttrack Fiction* (digital shorts). His stories have appeared in 65 journals. He has received six Pushcart Prize nominations, is a Commonwealth Prize shortlisted author, and the winner of the John Gilgun Fiction Award.

JACK STEWART

Jack Stewart was educated at the University of Alabama and Emory University. From 1992-95 he was a Brittain Fellow at The Georgia Institute of Technology. His work has appeared in *Poetry, The American Literary Review, The Dark Horse Review, The Southern Humanities Review,* and other journals and anthologies, most recently in *New Welsh Reader* and *Image.* He lives in Coconut Creek, Florida.

DIANA TOKAJI

Diana Tokaji is a writer and choreographer (London, San Francisco, Washington DC). Her poetry has appeared in *Bellevue Literary* and *The New Guard* (2019 finalist), and her essays and articles in trade journals, anthologies, and feminist and parenting presses. Forthcoming are her complete essay collection; her memoir, *Six Women in a Cell;* and her resource book, *Surviving Assault: Words that Rock & Quiet & Tell the Truth.*

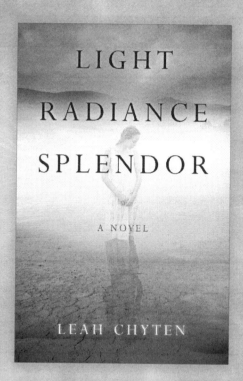

FOSTERING PEACE THROUGH LITERATURE & ART

SUBMIT YOUR WRITING

FOR POSSIBLE PUBLICATION IN TIFERET

We are always on the lookout for well-written, engaging, and hopefully consciousness-raising poetry and prose. Our editors carefully review each submission and selections are chosen for each issue.

Tiferet will be accepting submissions for our annual Writing Contest from JANUARY 1, 2020– MARCH 31, 2020. Awards of $500 are given to the winning submissions in each of three categories: Poetry, Fiction, and Nonfiction.

Visit http://tiferetjournal.com frequently for updates on submission dates and guidelines.

SUBMIT YOUR AD

Our readers, fans, followers and friends are interested in writing, spirituality, and promoting tolerance.

If you would like to advertise a product or service that is appropriate and relevant, please contact Lisa at lisa@ tiferetjournal.com. She can tell you more about the opportunities available to you in our print and digital issues, newsletter, Facebook and Twitter promotions, radio show—hosting, and more.

Made in the USA
Lexington, KY
26 November 2019